Young Burns

Young Burns

Tony Bonning

Illustrated by Gillian Alexander

WAVERLEY
BOOKS

YOUNG CLASSICS

ACKNOWLEDGEMENTS

My thanks to Russell Bryden and Lesley Garbutt of Kirkcudbright Library and Elinor Clark of Burns Cottage and Museum for their kind assistance in the research for this book.

TONY BONNING

Text copyright © 2006, Tony Bonning
Illustration copyright © 2006, Gillian Alexander

The moral rights of the author and illustrator have been asserted

Young Classics is a trademark of Waverley Books Ltd

Published 2006 by Waverley Books Ltd,
New Lanark, Scotland

ISBN 10: 1 902407 36 9
ISBN 13: 978 1 902407 36 4

Printed and bound in Poland

POLSKABOOK

DEDICATION

Dedicated to Robin Baird, who could always recite better, so made me work harder.

CONTENTS

STEP BACK IN TIME

Imagine going to school for only two or three years. Sounds good, doesn't it? But what if when you did, you had to walk all the way there, perhaps for miles, and barefoot? If you were very lucky, you might get an old pair of your father's cast-offs for the winter – well, for the frosty mornings anyway. Maybe not so good, after all.

What if, after your few years of schooling, you had to start work at the crack of dawn? Then work all day until sunset doing manual labour such as ploughing – not with a tractor, but driving a horse-drawn plough in all kinds of weather. On the days it was just too wet to plough, you might have to thresh the corn, milk the cows and goats, or repair fences and dry-stone walls.

THE WINTRY WIND EXTENDS HIS BLAST, AND HAIL AND RAIN DOES BLOW; OR THE STORMY NORTH SENDS DRIVING FORTH THE BLINDING SLEET AND SNOW.

All of a sudden going to school seems like fun by comparison – well almost! For young Robert Burnes this daily graft, grind and discomfort was the reality of his early life and times. If, for a moment, you think there's been a mix up and someone else has crept into our story, don't worry, he hasn't. If you think there's a spelling mistake in his surname, there isn't (as you will see below and on page 49) and this takes us back to the beginning of our fascinating story. Let us step back in time to over 200 years ago.

Birth of a genius

Robert, Robin or Rab, as he was sometimes called, was born in a modest countryside dwelling built by his father, William Burnes. In the straw thatch of the roof above his head, rats scuttled and squeaked and the room was lit by candle. It was the 25th day of January in the year 1759 and the weather was cold, bleak and stormy.

The smells that surrounded him were of homespun clothes and blankets, peat smoke, the hard earth and stone of the floor, boiled kail and porridge. Not forgetting

⊙⊙ Fast Facts

The greatest Scot

In the year 2000, the people of Scotland were asked to decide who was the greatest Scot who had ever lived. Their choice was none other than Robert Burns, national hero and world renowned bard.

the unmistakable reek of urine and manure from the animals in the room next door!

The first sounds Robert Burnes would have heard would have been the sweet singing voice of his handsome mother Agnes, the kindly voice of his proud father and, from out of the utterly black night, the howl of the winter wind blowing over the small village of Alloway, in rural south-west Scotland.

Later Robert would claim that the howling wind blew in on him the gift of writing and even referred to this in a poem that he wrote about himself, 'Rantin, Rovin Robin'. The less romantic truth is that some days later the wind blew down the end of the family's humble home and Robert and his mother had to seek refuge with a neighbour.

The day after the baby's birth there was a brief calm in the weather that allowed his father to ride into the nearby town of Ayr and bring back a minister to baptise the newly born infant. It was the tradition in those days to baptise a child as early as possible because of the high level of death in early childhood. It was generally believed that if a child died before being baptised it would be taken by the Devil down into the depths of Hell, or suffer the equally unpleasant fate of being doomed to wander the earth as a lost spirit.

⊙⊙ Fast Facts

The Kilmarnock Edition

Burns's first volume of poems, *Poems, Chiefly in the Scottish Dialect*, sometimes referred to as *The Kilmarnock Edition* because of where it was published and printed, came out on 31 July 1786. The publisher and printer was John Wilson. Robert Burns was just 27 years old and had already written, with the exception of 'Tam o'Shanter' and his songs, most of his greatest works.

Hard work and hard luck

After Robert's birth there would have been little rest for his mother, Agnes Broun or Brown, to give her maiden name. When his father went off to work as head gardener on the nearby country estate of Doonholm, the baby would have been wrapped in a plaidie or blanket and tied to his mother's back. She would then set about the day's work of looking after their croft or smallholding.

When Robert's father had first leased the six and a half acres surrounding their home it was to start a market gardening business; he even called the site New Gardens. Despite William's ambitions and hard work, the business did not succeed and instead it was run as a croft for the family's own use.

In Alloway in 1759 there was no village shop to buy provisions and supermarkets were a futuristic invention almost 200 years away. In those times working-class people usually grew their own food or starved. The Burnes family kept cows, goats, sheep and chickens.

NOTICE
SHOP NOT OPEN
UNTIL NEXT CENTURY.
HAVE A NICE DAY!

Beside the house was a kitchen garden or kailyard – so called because the main crop was usually kail. A member of the cabbage family, kail nowadays is used mainly for animal feed but back in the dim and distant past it was a vital ingredient of the staple diet of poor people in Scotland.

In the kailyard the family would also grow leeks, beans and herbs – potatoes and turnips were still quite rare. The rest of the land would be used as pasture for grazing the few animals they owned and to grow flax, barley and oats. Flax was used for making linen clothes, barley for making soups and the oats for making mainly porridge or 'crowdie', another mouth-watering mixture of oatmeal and water.

Soon young Robert would have been toddling barefoot after his mother as she searched for hens' eggs or milked the cows to make butter and cheese. Any spare home-grown products would be taken to Ayr on market days and sold or exchanged for other goods.

At this time, ships from the Far East and the West Indies regularly sailed into various ports on the River Clyde, laden with tea, sugar and spices, and sometimes these would be available at the market. (There was even a movement at the time to ban tea, as some people believed it was a bad influence!)

Tall tales

Eighteen months after Robert's birth a brother, Gilbert, was born and it would have been his turn to be wrapped in the plaidie and join his mother and older brother in the daily activities in and around their home.

In the evening, the boys would watch as their mother worked a spinning wheel to make yarn from the sheep's wool or flax she had gathered. The yarn would be taken to a local weaver to make cloth from which Robert's mother would then make clothes, mainly for herself and Robert's father. Robert's and Gilbert's clothes would have been made out of their parent's old and well-worn garments.

Robert's mother would spin other yarns also – stories! Agnes was born in Carrick, now called South Ayrshire, where many people still spoke Gaelic and storytelling was very much part of the local culture. Television, radio, record or CD players weren't around back then, of course. In time

Robert would learn to play the violin, but for the moment it was the voice of his mother telling folk-tales, or singing the ballads and songs of old Scotland, that echoed through their small house.

Rock on Rabbie!

Rock or pop music didn't exist in the 18th century, of course, but Burns was a superstar of his era – a mega-celebrity who became as famous for his exploits as for his poetry. After the publication of his first edition of poems, copies of the book found their way to Edinburgh where they caused a great stir.

Encouraged by the glowing reviews, Burns cancelled his imminent emigration to Jamaica and instead rode a pony to the capital. Not the quickest of journeys but a worthwhile one. On his arrival, he was greeted and treated in much the same way as a famous music or film star would be treated today.

A legend in his lifetime, Burns's talent has stood the test of time, even in the fickle and fast-changing world of popular music. In recent years many Scottish musicians and singers have rediscovered Burns, reinterpreting his songs and delighting new fans.

Home truths

There was no such thing as a free lunch, or a free breakfast or dinner come to that, when Burns was growing up. Everyone, even little children, had to pitch in and do their bit to help the family scratch a living and survive. It would not have been long before Robert learned the essential skills of milking, weeding the garden and mucking out the animal stalls, which in those days were in the room next to where the family lived.

The house was initially built as a 'but and ben', which was a small, two-roomed building. The family lived, cooked, ate and slept in one room – the ben. The animals slept in the other – the but. While the close accommodation guaranteed a rather strong aroma throughout the house, it also ensured extra heat in the freezing winters of the time. Later Robert's father, William, would build an extension to the house for the animals and give the growing family an extra room. (Robert's two sisters, Agnes and Annabella were also born at Alloway.)

Like children the world over, Robert and his brother found time for fun and games, running around outdoors and playing together. They no doubt also had the occasional argument and falling out, just like siblings the world over. Those carefree times are famously described in one of Burns's most famous songs that is now accepted as a world anthem – 'Auld Lang Syne'. The song is also an anthem to the pleasures of childhood.

Most likely Robert also learned a few country skills such as 'guddling' or catching fish by hand and snaring rabbits. We know that he had a general dislike of the cruelty that hunters can inflict on their fellow creatures but poverty and hunger are even crueller.

JUST HINGING ABOOT!

In the autumn, after the family had harvested the barley and oats grown in their fields, the children would trek with their mother across the countryside looking for crab apples, brambles, rosehips, elderberries and other wild fruit to make jams and cordials.

Early inspirations

Another childhood pastime would have been exploring his neighbourhood, which in young Burns's case consisted mainly of countryside stretching as far as the eye could see. In time his explorations would have led to the old church in the village, Kirk Alloway, which is immortalised in Robert Burns's most famous poem, 'Tam o' Shanter'.

Kirk Alloway was associated with a number of local folk tales and would have been a scary place in those superstitious times. Childhood imagination being what it is, in the mind of young Burns there would have been devils and bogles lurking behind every gravestone. To make matters worse, Robert's parents employed a home help by the name of Betty Davidson. Betty had an endless store of folk and fairy tales which she herself believed as truth.

These tales had a lasting effect on Robert and even as a man he had difficulty in throwing off the fears planted in him by Betty's stories. They also had another and far-reaching effect: they planted the seeds of poetry in his fertile imagination.

Lessons for life

Escaping hardship during Robert Burns's lifetime was difficult and even more so without an education. Robert's father had benefitted from a bit of an education himself and was determined that his family would be better prepared for the world. When a school opened nearby in 1765, Robert and Gilbert were enrolled.

Unfortunately (or fortunately depending on which side of the desk you were sitting) the school remained open for only a few weeks. In frustration, William Burnes convinced some other local parents to join him in hiring and paying for a teacher of their own. As a result our hero began to develop the skills that all great writers and we mere mortals need: the ability to read and write.

Famous figure

Statues of Robert Burns can be found and admired right across the world. The first statue was erected in Ayr in 1891. A smaller copy of this statue stands in the Sorbonne in Paris. It was hidden away during World War II to prevent its capture by the Nazis.

WE HAVE WAYS OF MAKING YOU TALK. WHERE IS THE STATUE?

More importantly, the young teacher, John Murdoch, and Robert's father inspired young Burns to develop an early love of words. At the age of six the fledgling bard was reading books that would defy the ability of someone twice his age nowadays. Large portions of the Bible, hymns and poetry were committed to memory. Poems were rewritten as prose to make sure Robert and his classmates knew the meaning of what they were reading. And this was before rubbers were invented!

Summing up success

It's said that genius is 2% inspiration and 98% perspiration. Take a look at a copy of the *Complete Works of Robert Burns* in any library or bookshop and you'll see just how much perspiration was required. And this was before deodorant was invented! Remember also that he had a farm to run and a family to raise at the same time.

CHILDHOOD EXPERIENCES

TWO YEARS EDUCATION

LIFE TIME OF INSPIRATION

Weekends not allowed!

A school day in the 18th century could start at seven in the morning and last until six in the evening for six days a week, with a Sabbath School after church on Sunday.

The idea of such long days would frighten any child in the 21st century and scare the living daylights out of your teacher. But this was one reason Burns was so well educated in the short time that he went to school. Another reason was that John Murdoch was a dedicated and excellent teacher.

The writing implements that the schoolchildren would have used were chalk on a slate or a home-made goose-feather pen and ink. The ink would have been made with soot from the fire.

Another tool of the classroom was the famed hornbook. This was a small, paddle-shaped board which was covered in paper and inscribed with the numbers one to ten, the alphabet in capital and lower case letters, and the Lord's Prayer. The board was covered in a thin, transparent sheet of cowhorn to protect the paper – which, funnily enough, is where the term hornbook comes from!

On a different note

Robert Burns was said to have a problem with singing. According to his teacher, John Murdoch, his voice was 'dull and untuneable'. His pupil knew the words perfectly well but couldn't get his voice round the melody.

For someone who grew up to write or rewrite the words to many of Scotland's ancient and often complicated melodies and who became a competent player of the violin, this poor report would seem rather strange. The answer may be simply this: ask even a reasonable singer to sing in a key not suited to their voice and it will probably come out like a croak.

Children sing in a higher range and find the keys suited to most adult voices difficult, if not impossible. If John Murdoch expected Robert to sing in the same key as him, he was probably asking the impossible.

So, if anyone tries to tell you that Robert Burns couldn't sing, tell them to change their tune!

What's the story?

As soon as he could read, our young hero developed a passion for books. His early favourites were the stories of the great Scottish patriot, William Wallace, and of Hannibal who crossed the Alps on an elephant in AD 218 and defeated the armies of ancient Rome. Such was the effect of these stirring tales that when the army recruiters came to town, Robert would strut and march behind the recruiting drum wishing himself big enough to be a soldier.

Most, if not all, of the books that young Burns read were written in English and included the works of the great poets of the day, including Shakespeare, Dryden and Milton. At the time there was a great attempt to suppress the Scots language and only a few popular Scottish poets, such as Allan Ramsay and Robert Ferguson, used it to great effect.

But Scots was the everyday language of Burns and the beauty of it lies in its sense of place. It is the language of country folk, farmers and peasants, and in this respect is highly descriptive; though it is largely unintelligible to the modern ear. While we're on the subject, it's an insult to the Scots language and the Scottish people to suggest that Oxford English is somehow superior. It's just a dialect of English and no more superior than Geordie or Liverpudlian!

We know that young Robert didn't write his first piece until he was 15 years old, but it's easy to imagine him running poetry through his mind, reciting it to his parents and very likely writing parodies that gave voice to his keen sense of humour. Perhaps he even translated them into everyday Scots for the sake of his mother and Betty Davidson. Whatever the truth of his early attempts, it was writing in Scots or Lallans (Lowlands) that would make his name as a poet.

๏ð Fast Facts

Say that again!

The language we today call Scots was at one time referred to as Inglis – the original Scots people actually spoke Gaelic. Inglis grew from the language spoken by the Angles who came from Northern Germany and settled in Norfolk, in what is still called East Anglia today, and was the original Englaland or England. To confuse you even more, the original Scotland was present day Northern Ireland.

Farming folk

In 1765 Robert's ambitious father decided to become a farmer. Imagine the excitement! Being a farmer was something special and important in local communities and farming was a cornerstone of rural life. To six-year-old Robert and his brother and sisters it must have seemed as great an adventure as riding elephants over the Alps with Hannibal.

The family gave up their small croft in Alloway and moved two miles east to the 90-acre farm of Mount Oliphant. It was a brave move, for the rent was £40 a year – a very large sum for the time and a great deal more than the land was worth. Sadly, it would ultimately bring the family a bitter harvest.

Visiting the area today, it's hard to believe that in Robert Burns's time it was bleak moorland. The pleasant fields, hedges and trees give the land a feeling of gentleness and softness. Yet even in Burns's childhood, Mount Oliphant on a good day must have seemed like paradise.

DREICH DAY AGAIN!

In bad weather, however, it must have seemed the worst place on earth, with cold wind sliding over the open moor and sloping ribbons of rain sweeping in from the sea. It was during these harsh conditions that Robert had to walk behind the plough while his father led the pulling team of four horses. The job often required three people and young Gilbert would have had the job of keeping the nose of the plough in the ground with a long pole.

Robert later wrote in a letter to a friend, Dr Moore, about his early experiences of farming:

We lived very poorly: I was a dextrous ploughman for my age; and the next oldest to me was a brother who could drive the plough very well, and help me thresh the corn. A novel writer might view these scenes with satisfaction; but so did not I.

To work through an endless day when you are wet, cold and weary before midday is torture to most. To a child it is almost beyond endurance.

Undoubtedly it taught Robert how to be tough and how to endure. And endure it he did, boy and man. It would also be the cause of bringing him to an early grave through rheumatics – an inflammation or swelling of the heart almost certainly contracted through continuous soakings in childhood.

Ill advice

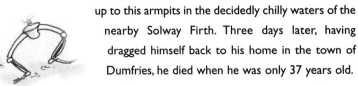

You've probably heard the expression 'kill or cure' – usually when someone is trying to persuade you to swallow a mouthful of vile medicine. Unfortunately for Robert Burns, his doctor's orders definitely didn't cure him and very possibly helped to kill him.

After many years of poor health, brought on in part by too much hard work in his childhood and teens, by 1796 Robert was a shadow of his former self. The financial worry of trying to raise his growing family on his salary as a customs man and the little income he received from his writings, added to his plight.

Desperate to regain his health and strength, in July 1796 he followed the advice of his friend and doctor, William Maxwell, by first bathing in local spring waters. To make matters worse, he then plunged himself into the second part of the treatment by wading up to this armpits in the decidedly chilly waters of the nearby Solway Firth. Three days later, having dragged himself back to his home in the town of Dumfries, he died when he was only 37 years old.

Working the land

The first job the family would have tackled after moving to Mount Oliphant would have been to build a network of dykes 'inby', or close to the farm, to keep their animals off the crops. There were few or no fences or hedges in those days. The 'outby' fields were usually left as pasture where the animals were herded and fed under supervision.

In the inby fields, crops like oats, barley and flax were grown. There were no drains to take water off the field and so they were often boggy. The solution was to organise fields in a runrig system. Soil was banked up in long narrow strips or rigs. This made the soil deeper and water gathered between the rigs. Manure went on top and then the crop was planted.

It was a very inefficient system of farming and coupled with the poor, thin soil of Mount Oliphant, crop failure and poor harvests were a regular occurrence.

Food for thought

Apart from an animal dying from illness, the only time meat would have been available to the family would have been just once a year at Martinmass (11 November) when, traditionally, any cows not to be kept over winter were slaughtered. The meat was then dried or salted to stop it going bad over the winter. Cruel though it may seem, the simple reason for killing healthy animals was that there wasn't enough feed to keep them all alive over the winter months – there was little enough feed for people.

That said, the diet of simple Scottish country folk at that time was not as bad as is sometimes made out. The main part of the diet was oats, either by way of porridge or oatcakes and bannocks, which provided carbohydrate. Protein would come mainly from cheese, milk and eggs, and vitamins and iron from the green vegetables of the kailyard.

The main drinks were milk and buttermilk, or swats, which was made by steeping fine oatmeal and husks in water for over a week. What settled at the bottom was given to the chickens while the liquid was left to stand for another week to ferment. What then settled at the bottom was called sowens, which was eaten, and the liquid was called the swats. It was very popular, even with children; probably because it could sometimes be slightly alcoholic (hic!).

MENU

Porridge
Oatcakes
or
Bannocks

Cheese
or
Eggs

Green Vegetables
fresh from the
Kailyard

Washed down
with Milk,
Buttermilk or
Swats!!

Learning on the job

Despite living further away from the village school, Robert and Gilbert continued being taught by John Murdoch in Alloway after moving to Mount Oliphant. But that came to end in early 1768 when the schoolmaster took up a new job in Dumfries. The lack of a teacher and the fact that Robert's father couldn't afford hired labour meant that Robert began his working life in earnest at only nine years of age.

Although he was working the livelong day in a way that would now be unacceptable and probably considered nothing less than a kind of slavery, it didn't prevent young Burns from developing his mind. As they worked, Robert's father ensured that their discussions involved learning more about the world. In the evening, the family, with the exception of mother Agnes who couldn't read, would gather round the lamp and stick

their heads into books. The girls were also encouraged to join in as, unusually for the times, their forward-thinking father had taught them to read.

What did they read? Anything and everything they could get their hands on. This was no easy task as books were rare, expensive and difficult to obtain. Much of what was read was religion based, with snappy titles like: *New History of the Holy Bible from the Beginnings of the World to the Establishment of Christianity; Astro-Theology or a Demonstration on the Being and Attributes of God* and *The Wisdom of God Manifest in the Works of the Creation.*

Not exactly light reading for a young boy, nowadays these books would prove virtually impossible to wade through even for an adult. Nonetheless, Robert devoured them from cover to cover, even by candlelight!

⊙⊙ Fast Facts

Wrong book, right result

Through a happy accident an uncle, who was living with the family at the time, arrived back from Ayr with a copy of *The Complete Letter Writer.* The uncle had originally planned to buy an arithmetic book. The book he bought instead contained a collection of letters by some of the great writers of the age. It created in young Burns the desire to be an excellent letter writer, which he undoubtedly became.

Thou shalt not, never ever!

As can be seen from the sample list of books read by the Burns family, religion played a major part in the life of the young poet. Although the Catholic faith was still practised in Scotland, it was the Presbyterian or Protestant faith with its cold eye on life that dominated the time. Presbyterianism was then divided into two camps: the Auld Licht and the New Licht – the Old Light and the New Light.

The Auld Licht still held to hardline Calvinism. Followers of the preacher, John Calvin, believed in a vengeful God, hellfire and damnation. Put simply: you followed the Bible word for word or you would roast in Hell forever. Dancing was the work of the Devil, singing anything other than hymns was heavily frowned upon and if you missed church on Sunday you were liable to be fined or imprisoned. In earlier times, advocates of the Auld Licht caused mayhem in the countryside by accusing many simple country folk of witchcraft.

DANCING AND SINGING! DO YOU THINK YOU'RE HERE ON EARTH TO ENJOY YOURSELF, LADDIE?

With the introduction of the New Licht, things became a little easier but even their beliefs were still worse than strict by modern standards. Not attending church could still get you into big trouble and bad behaviour would have you sitting on the cutty stool – a short-legged stool on which the guilty, to their embarrassment, would have to sit in front of the congregation. During Sunday services, which could last for up to three hours, scoldings and rebukes from the minister would rain down on the poor victim. Our young Robert was to spend many an hour on the stool or, as he called it, 'the creepy-chair', bearing the brunt of the minister's scorn and the congregation's disapproval.

⊙ⓓ Fast Facts

Grave details

Robert Burns is buried in a magnificent mausoleum – a grand tomb – in St Michael's Kirkyard, Dumfries, along with his long-suffering wife, Jean Armour, who died 38 years after her husband. His father, William, is buried at the entrance to Kirk Alloway and his mother, Agnes, is buried in East Lothian where she moved with Robert's brother, Gilbert.

Back to school

When Robert was 13 years old in 1772, the boys' former teacher, John Murdoch, paid a visit to the farm and casually remarked on the poor quality of their handwriting. This prompted their father to send them, week about, to the parish school of Dalrymple for handwriting classes during the summer.

The school was two and a half miles south-east of Mount Oliphant, with the boys having to walk there and back. As can be seen from Burns's original letters, the five-mile walk was worth it, for his handwriting improved enormously. We can only hope it did the same for Gilbert!

The following year, Robert was sent by his father to study under John Murdoch, who had moved back to Ayr. He was only there a week when he had to return to help with the harvest at home. After the harvest, Robert returned to Ayr for another two weeks, during which time he also studied French.

In his autobiographical letter to Dr Moore, Burns describes vividly his dress and appearance at the time, using the wonderfully descriptive word, 'clouterly'. A clout or cloot is a patch, rag or dishcloth.

Coming from a family who were continuously on the edge of real poverty, it must have been a source of embarrassment for the young Burns to go to a wealthy town such as Ayr. It says something of his great personality that he could report:

My young superiors never insulted the clouterly appearance of my ploughboy carcase, the two extremes of which (his head and feet) *were often exposed to all the inclemencies of all the seasons.*

Only the coldest heart could not feel a little pity for the poor people of those hard and unforgiving times.

⊙⊙ Fast Facts

Spell check

After his childhood education ended, young Burns returned to farming life or, as he put it, to

> 'the chearless gloom of a hermit with the unceasing toil of a galley slave.'

If you're eagle-eyed, you'll have spotted an apparent mis-spelling of the word *cheerless*. In those days, some words were still spelled as a matter of choice.

Top marks

His final studies with John Murdoch at the age of 14 signalled the end of his school years and all the tuition Robert Burns ever received in writing and grammar. What enabled him to achieve so much with so little formal education? What made him so different from other boys who experienced a similar level of schooling, and even those who spent many more years studying at the best universities under the guidance of the finest academics?

AWAY YE GO AND DINNA BUG ME!

The difference was that Robert Burns wanted to learn. He was a devoted pupil and, although he had a great deal of intelligence, he also possessed two essential qualities: the ability to work hard and determination. He could have been the most intelligent person in the world but without these special qualities, today we would be asking 'Robert who?'

⊙⊙ Fast Facts

Enduring themes

Burns was certainly not the first writer to address the plight of humanity. Other great scribes and thinkers such as William Shakespeare and Tom Paine, who wrote *The Rights of Man,* strode the world stage before him. (Burns wrote a response in favour of the opposite sex, entitled 'The Rights of Woman', around the same time.) But it is widely acknowledged that the poetry of Robert Burns has contributed greatly to our continuing awareness of the need to respect and get along with our fellow human beings.

Devilish behaviour

Although the lease of the farm was what Robert later called 'a ruinous bargain', his father, William, unable to find or afford another and better farm, extended the lease for a further six years. It was during this time that Robert first began writing poetry; or, as he said, 'committed the sin of 'RHYME.'

The idea that writing poetry could be a sin seems quite ridiculous to us now and perhaps he was making a joke. However, there were many devoutly religious people who would have considered this harmless pleasure a sin. It was acceptable to write hymns or works on the Bible. Anything else was the Devil's work.

GO ON, BE A DEVIL. WRITE ANOTHER!

Tale of the tail

In 1789, Robert Burns met and became firm friends with the artist, Captain Francis Grose, who was travelling through Scotland sketching famous places. Robert suggested to Grose that he include Kirk Alloway among his drawings. Grose agreed on condition that Robert wrote a poem to go with the drawing. The bard gave him a choice of three stories and Grose decided on the one about a drunken farmer who interrupts a witches' dance and, when he's chased, his horse loses its tail. This story was a common tale in south-west Scotland.

Kirk Alloway had a reputation as a haunt of the devil after a young bull was trapped in it. Two young girls passing the ruin heard the bull bellowing, saw a pair of horns at the window and fled thinking it was 'Auld Hornie' – the Devil – himself.

Robert also had an acquaintance from his time spent at Kirkoswald, Douglas Graham who, along with his shoemaker friend, John Davidson or Souter Johnnie, would get drunk after a day at the market. He would then ride the fifteen miles from Ayr to Shanter Farm in Carrick, passing Kirk Alloway on the way.

With all this in mind, Robert Burns created what is arguably one of the great poems of all time and, although written in thick Scots, it is still a joy to the ear – the epic 'Tam o' Shanter'.

Fancy that

What makes a young man or woman turn to writing poetry and song? The most common reason is becoming aware of the opposite sex; and so it was for young Burns. Most of the time the only people that Robert saw on the farm were his family. Come harvest time, however, the farmers of the district and their workers helped each other to bring in the crop as quickly as possible in case of bad weather.

During one such harvest, Robert met with a young woman who we know, from the song she inspired, as 'Handsome Nell'. There's often argument as to who she really was, but it's likely that she was Helen or Nelly Blair, a servant lass from a neighbouring house. But let Robert tell the story in his own words ...

You know our country custom of coupling a man and a woman together as Partners in the labors of Harvest. In my fifteenth autumn, my Partner was a bewitching creature who just counted an autumn less. My scarcity of English denies me the power of doing her justice in that language; but you know the Scotch idiom, She was a bonie, sweet, sonsie lass. In short, she altogether unwittingly to herself, initiated me into a certain delicious passion, which in spite of acid disappointments, gin horse prudence, and book-worm Philosophy, I hold to be the first of human joys, our chiefest pleasure here below. How she caught the contagion I can't say: you medical folks talk much of infection by breathing the same air, the touch, etc. but I never told her expressedly that I loved her. Indeed I did not know well myself why I liked so much to loiter behind with her when returning in the evening from our labors; why the tones of her voice made my heartstrings thrill like an Aeolian harp; and particularly why my heart beat such a furious ratann when I looked and fingered over her hand, to pick out the nettle-stings and thistles. Among her other love-inspiring qualifications, she sung sweetly; and 'twas her favourite reel to which I attempted giving an embodied vehicle in rhyme. I was not so presumtious as to imagine that I could make verses like printed ones, composed by men who had Greek and Latin; but my girl sung a song which was said to be composd by a small country laird's son, on one of his father's maids with whom he was in love; and I saw no reason why I might not rhyme as well as he; for excepting that he could smear sheep, and cast peats, his father living in the moorlands, he had no more scholar-craft than myself.

Thus with me began Love and Poesy(poetry); which at times have been my only, and till within the last twelvemonth have been my highest enjoyment.

Robt. Burns

๐๏ Fast Facts

Burns Supper

The first Burns Supper was held in honour of the poet at Burns Cottage in Alloway on 21 July 1801 – the fifth anniversary of his death. The group of nine Ayrshire gentlemen agreed to meet the following January, and so began the tradition. Nowadays, there are over 1,000 Burns clubs and societies throughout the world, each commemorating and celebrating the poet's unique contribution to literature.

Career move

In the summer of 1775, when he was 16 years old, Robert's father sent him to Kirkoswald, a small village ten miles south of Mount Oliphant, to study geometry and mathematics. The main purpose was to learn how to be a land surveyor – a job that would have given the young man a career, not to mention the possibility of improving the land on the family farm.

Although Robert worked hard under the tuition of the hard-nosed dominie or teacher, Hugh Rodger, mathematics was not to his liking. However, his time away from home taught him a few other lessons in the school of life: the habits of the tavern and that there were other girls in the world beside Handsome Nell.

Margaret Thompson, a local girl, inspired him to pen the words to one of his earliest songs, 'Now Westlin Winds'. Written when he was still a mere 16 year old, it paints a vivid picture of two things dear to Robert's poetic heart – nature and love.

There is something else of special interest to us about his time studying in Kirkoswald. It was there he met Douglas Graham, his model for Tam o' Shanter, and his wife, Helen. In fact, all the people mentioned by name or profession in the poem lived in and around Kirkoswald. It would be another 20 years before they would be committed to paper and immortality, but this underlines a key message in the life of young Burns and, indeed, our own lives. What we do in childhood and the experiences we have then inspire and prepare us for our future as adults.

⊙ð **Fast Facts**

Just joking

When in Kirkoswald, young Burns was walking uphill on Kirk Brae. The minister passing by enquired where he was going. Burns gave the reply, 'As you can see Sir, I am proceeding heavenwards.' The minister was left to consider in which direction he was going. Hell?

Personal best

Considering his international fame and revered status, it seems hard to believe that Robert Burns only received a total of around two-and-a-half years of schooling. Okay, the teaching was far more intense than today and there weren't the same distractions around and John Murdoch was, by all accounts, an extraordinary teacher. Add to that the dedicated guidance of his father, William, and Robert's time with Hugh Rodger and we can see that young Burns's education may have been short but it was highly effective.

But what really made it work was that Robert continued to learn long after he left school. He was what we call an 'autodidact'. In other words, he was self-taught. In the end it's up to each of us to strive to be the best we can. That's the lesson of all great people. It's in every one of us to do well – or not if we don't even try.

For Robert Burns the hardest of lives was thrown at him and, though he died young, he produced some of the most enduring literature of humanity. He has been a great inspiration to poets, writers, musicians and people from all walks of life, right up to the present day. His words ring true down the years and make us think about the world we live in and how we treat our fellow creatures and fellow human beings.

Not bad for a wee raggedy boy who trod barefoot to school auld lang syne!

∞ Fast Facts

Squeak up

The title of the classic novel, *Of Mice and Men*, by American writer, John Steinbeck, is a direct quote from one of Burns's best loved poems, 'To a Mouse':

> 'The best-laid schemes of mice and men
> Gang aft agley.' (often go wrong)

Myths about Burns

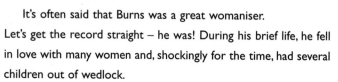

Even in his own lifetime myths surrounded
Robert Burns. Here are just a few.

It's often said that Burns was a great womaniser.
Let's get the record straight – he was! During his brief life, he fell
in love with many women and, shockingly for the time, had several
children out of wedlock.

Another myth was that he was at worst an alcoholic and at
best a hard drinker. Firstly, heavy drinking was the norm in the 18th
century and Burns was probably no worse than other men and
even some women! That he declined drink when others around
him were getting heavily intoxicated has been recorded in his
defence. But the strongest argument in his favour is that if he been
an excessive drinker, it would have been impossible to produce the
quantity and quality of work he did in his short life. The two simply
do not go together.

Yet another myth was that he composed all the songs in his
collected works – the works are often referred to as the
Songs of Robert Burns. Most were, in fact, old Scottish songs that had
been around for many, sometimes hundreds of, years. The bard
collected these songs on his travels around Scotland and often

reworked, revised or otherwise improved the words; the
melodies remained as he found them. In many instances, he
was inspired to compose new lyrics.

The man's a man

We will stop the story of our hero's childhood here. By now Robert Burnes was on the threshold of becoming a man. The family would alter their surname from Burnes to Burns, never imagining how famous it would become worldwide. As an adult, Burns would work as a farmer and an exciseman or customs officer.

In a few years, he would write and publish some of the greatest poems of all time. Poems that would be read the world over, with lines that people would use in everyday conversation without even realising who had written them.

In time Burns would go on to write what may be considered one of the greatest narrative poems, 'Tam o'Shanter', and one of the most stirring anthems about Scottish history, 'Scots Wha Hae'. He would re-write 'Auld Lang Syne', the world's anthem at New Year celebrations, and save hundreds of ancient Scottish songs from disappearing forever.

In his day he was the equivalent of a rock star and movie superstar all rolled into one. He was the toast of Scottish society and a friend of many of the great and good of the age.

Robert Burns is, without doubt, one of the greatest Scotsmen who have ever lived and one of the truly great human beings in the history of humankind. Yet his beginnings were much the same as most human beings, if a little harder and certainly humbler than many.

We may not have it in us to be another Robert Burns. But if we take a leaf or two from his book and show hard work and determination, perhaps we can have a worthwhile and good life. We may even, like Robert Burns, help make this world a better place to live in.

It's worth trying, an' a' that!

SELECTED WORKS

During his brief but busy lifetime, Robert Burns wrote hundreds of poems and songs – too many to include in this book. Instead you'll find a selection of the bard's most famous and much loved works.

Think of it is an introduction to Burns – a taster of his unique talent for turning words, observations, passions, beliefs and experiences into miniature masterpieces. Who knows, you may even develop a lifelong appetite for a true literary great!

A word to the wise

When reading the works of Robert Burns there will be many unfamiliar words. It's important to understand the words otherwise the piece will make as much sense as a secret code. But breaking the code is easy, with a little help. In the case of unusual Scottish words, you'll find a glossary on the right-hand margin of each poem or song. If the word is not defined it's likely to be a Standard English word and can be found in any good English dictionary.

Handy hint: having a dictionary beside you whenever you read is a good habit to learn!

Love letters

Probably the last thing you'll want to read are love songs and poems that are full of soppy sentiments and toe-curling declarations. So we've put them first. In a few years they will, guaranteed, seem quite different, but for now – Yuk!

But wait a minute! What about the love we have for our parents, grandparents, brothers and sisters, aunts and uncles and so on? If we didn't have that, life would be pretty rotten. So maybe love does count in other ways as well.

Robert Burns was born into a very loving family. It was almost certainly this love that grew in him a giant heart and, in turn, expressed itself through love of nature, love for his fellow human beings and, as he reached manhood, love for the opposite sex.

A passionate person who often found the women he met inspirational and irresistible, Robert was the eternal romantic.

In that last respect he wrote one of the greatest love songs of all time, 'Ae Fond Kiss'. In fact, this and another of his beautiful songs, 'Ye Banks and Braes', are really about the loss of the one you love. Listen to many modern love songs and the subject is still the same: boy finds girl, boy loses girl and, with luck, he finds girl again – or vice versa.

All of which goes to prove that although they were written over 200 years ago, there are some songs and heart-felt emotions that never date.

HANDSOME NELL

O, once I lov'd a bonie lass,   *pretty*
Aye, and I love her still!   *Always*
And whilst that virtue warms my breast,
I'll love my handsome Nell.

As bonie lasses I hae seen,   *have*
And mony full as braw,   *many, beautiful*
But, for a modest gracefu' mien,
The like I never saw.

A bonie lass, I will confess,
Is pleasant to the e'e,   *eye*
But, without some better qualities,
She's no a lass for me.

But Nelly's looks are blithe and sweet,
And what is best of a',   *all*
Her reputation is complete
And fair without a flaw.

She dresses ay sae clean and neat,   *always so*
Both decent and genteel;
And then there's something in her gait
Gars ony dress look weel.   *Make any, well*

A gaudy dress and gentle air
May slightly touch the heart;
But it's innocence and modesty
That polishes the dart.

'Tis this in Nelly pleases me,
'Tis this enchants my soul;
For absolutely in my breast
She reigns without control.

NOW WESTLIN WINDS

A Song Composed in August

Now westlin winds and slaught'ring guns
Bring Autumn's pleasant weather;
The moorcock springs on whirring wings,
Amang the blooming heather: *Among*
Now waving grain, wide o'er the plain,
Delights the weary farmer;
And the moon shines bright, when I rove at night,
To muse upon my charmer.

The partridge loves the fruitful fells;
The plover loves the mountains;
The woodcock haunts the lonely dells;
The soaring hern the fountains: *heron*
Thro' lofty groves the cushat roves,   *wood-pigeon*
The path of man to shun it;
The hazel-bush o'erhangs the thrush
The spreading thorn the linnet.

Thus ev'ry kind their pleasure find,
The savage and the tender;
Some social join, and leagues combine,
Some solitary wander:
Avaunt, away, the cruel sway!
Tyrannic man's dominion;
The sportsman's joy, the murd'ring cry,
The flutt'ring, gory pinion!

But, Peggy dear, the ev'ning's clear,
Thick flies the skimming swallow;
The sky is blue, the fields in view,
All fading-green and yellow:
Come let us stray our gladsome way,
And view the charms of Nature;
The rustling corn, the fruited thorn,
And ev'ry happy creature.

We'll gently walk, and sweetly talk,
Till the silent moon shine clearly;
I'll grasp thy waist and, fondly prest,
Swear how I love thee dearly:
Nor vernal show'rs to budding flow'rs,
Not Autumn to the farmer,
So dear can be as thou to me,
My fair, my lovely charmer!

AE FOND KISS

Ae fond kiss, and then we sever;   *One*
Ae fareweel, and then for ever!
Deep in heart-wrung tears I'll pledge thee,
Warring sighs and groans I'll wage thee.

Who shall say that Fortune grieves him
While the star of hope she leaves him?
Me, nae cheerful twinkle lights me: *no*
Dark despair around benights me.

I'll ne'er blame my partial fancy,
Naething could resist my Nancy:
But to see her was to love her;
Love but her, and love forever.

Had we never lov'd sae kindly!
Had we never lov'd sae blindly!
Never met, or never parted,
We had ne'er been broken-hearted.

Fare thee weel, thou first and fairest!
Fare thee weel, thou best and dearest!
Thine be ilka joy and treasure,   *every*
Peace, Enjoyment, Love and Pleasure!

MY LUVE'S LIKE A RED, RED ROSE

Oh my luve's like a red, red rose,　　　　　　*love*
That's newly sprung in June;
Oh my luve's like the melodie,
That's sweetly play'd in tune.
As fair art thou, my bonie lass,
So deep in luve am I;
And I will luve thee still, my Dear,
Till a' the seas gang dry.　　　　　　　　　　*all, go*

Till a' the seas gang dry, my Dear,
And the rocks melt wi' the sun;　　　　　　　*with*
And I will luve thee still, my Dear,
While the sands o' life shall run.　　　　　　*of*
And fare thee weel, my only Luve!　　　　　　*well*
And fare thee weel a while!
And I will come again, my Luve,
Tho' it were ten thousand mile!

THE BANKS O' DOON

Ye banks and braes o' bonie Doon,   *of beautiful*
How can ye bloom sae fresh and fair?   *so*
How can ye chant, ye little birds,
And I sae weary fu' o' care!   *full*
Thou'll break my heart, thou warbling bird,
That wantons thro' the flowering thorn:
Thou minds me o' departed joys,
Departed never to return.

Aft hae I rov'd by bonie Doon,   *Often have*
To see the rose and woodbine twine;
And ilka bird sang o' its luve,   *each, love*
And fondly sae did I o' mine;
Wi' lightsome heart I pu'd a rose,   *With, pulled*
Fu' sweet upon its thorny tree!
And my fause luver staw my rose,   *false lover stole*
But ah! he left the thorn wi' me.

JOHN ANDERSON, MY JO

John Anderson, my jo, John,   *darling*
When we were first acquent;   *acquainted*
Your locks were like the raven,
Your bonie brow was brent;   *handsome, unwrinkled*
But now your brow is beld, John,   *bald*
Your locks are like the snaw;   *snow*
But blessings on your frosty pow,   *white head*
John Anderson, my jo.

John Anderson, my jo, John,
We clamb the hill thegither;   *climbed, together*
And mony a cantie day, John,   *many, happy*
We've had wi' ane anither: *with one another*
Now we maun totter down, John,   *must stagger*
And hand in hand we'll go,
And sleep thegither at the foot,
John Anderson, my jo.

CA' THE YOWES TO THE KNOWES

Chorus

Ca' the yowes to the knowes,	*Drive, ewes, knolls*
Ca' them where the heather grows	
Ca' them where the burnie rows,	*small stream runs*
My bonie Dearie.	

Hark, the mavis' evening sang	*thrush, song*
Sounding Clouden's woods amang;	*among*
Then a-fauldin let us gang,	*penning sheep, go*
My bonie Dearie.	

We'll gae down by Clouden side,	*go*
Thro' the hazels, spreading wide,	
O'er the waves that sweetly glide,	
To the moon sae clearly.	*so*

Yonder Clouden's silent towers,
Where, at moonshine's midnight hours,
O'er the dewy bending flowers,
Fairies dance sae cheery.

Ghaist nor bogle shalt thou fear;	*ghost, demon*
Thou 'rt to Love and Heaven sae dear,	
Nocht of ill may come thee near,	*Nothing*
My bonie Dearie.	

Fair and lovely as thou art,	
Thou hast stown my very heart;	*stolen*
I can die – but canna part,	*cannot*
My bonie Dearie.	

DUNCAN GRAY

Duncan Gray cam' here to woo,   *came*
Ha, ha, the wooing o' 't!   *of it*
On blythe Yule night when we were fou,   *drunk*
Ha, ha, the wooing o' 't.
Maggie coost her head fu high,   *tossed, full*
Look'd asklent and unco skeigh,   *disdainfully, unusually coy*
Gart poor Duncan stand abeigh;   *Made, aloof*
Ha, ha, the wooing o' 't!

Duncan fleech'd, and Duncan pray'd,   *wheedled*
Ha, ha, the wooing o' 't!
Meg was deaf as Ailsa Craig,
Ha, ha, the wooing o' 't!
Duncan sigh'd baith out and in,   *both*
Grat his e'en baith bleer't an' blin',   *Cried, eyes both blurred, blind*
Spak o' lowpin o're a linn;   *Spoke, leaping over, waterfall*
Ha, ha, the wooing o' 't!

Time and Chance are but a tide,
Ha, ha, the wooing o' 't!
Slighted love is sair to bide,   *hard, endure*
Ha, ha, the wooing o' 't!
'Shall I, like a fool,' quoth he,
'For a haughty hizzie die?   *hussy*
She may gae to – France for me!'
Ha, ha, the wooing o' 't!

How it comes let doctors tell,
Ha, ha, the wooing o' 't!
Meg grew sick as he grew hale,   *healthy*
Ha, ha, the wooing o' 't!
Something in her bosom wrings,
For relief a sigh she brings;
And O! her een, they spak sic things   *eyes, spoke such*
Ha, ha, the wooing o' 't!

Duncan was a lad o' grace,
Ha, ha, the wooing o' 't!
Maggie's was a piteous case,
Ha, ha, the wooing o' 't!
Duncan could na be her death,
Swelling pity smoor'd his wrath;   *smothered*
Now they're crouse and canty baith;   *proud, jolly*
Ha, ha, the wooing o' 't!

GREEN GROW THE RASHES, O!

Green grow the rashes, O!   *rushes (water plant)*
Green grow the rashes, O!
The sweetest hours that e'er I spend,
Are spent amang the lasses, O!   *among*

There's nought but care on every han'   *naught, hand*
In every hour that passes, O;
What signifies the life o' man,   *of*
An 'twere na for the lasses, O?   *And, not*

The warl'ly race may riches chase,   *worldly*
An' riches still may fly them, O;
An' though at last they catch them fast,
Their hearts can ne'er enjoy them, O.

But gi'e me a canny hour at e'en,   *give, evening*
My arms about my dearie, O,
An' warl'ly cares an' warl'ly men
May a' gae tapsalteerie, O!   *all go upsidedown*

For you sae douce, ye sneer at this,   *so sober / stuck up*
Ye're nought but senseless asses, O;
The wisest man the warl' e'er saw,
He dearly loved the lasses, O.

Auld Nature swears the lovely dears   *Old*
Her noblest work she classes, O;
Her 'prentice han' she tried on man,   *apprentice*
An' then she made the lasses, O.

OH, WERT THOU IN THE CAULD BLAST

Oh, wert thou in the cauld blast,   *cold*
On yonder lea, on yonder lea,
My plaidie to the angry airt, *tartan shawl, direction*
I'd shelter thee, I'd shelter thee;
Or did Misfortune's bitter storms
Around thee blaw, around thee blaw,   *blow*
Thy bield should be my bosom,   *shelter*
To share it a', to share it a'.   *all*

Or were I in the wildest waste,
Sae black and bare, sae black and bare,   *So*
The desert were a paradise,
If thou wert there, if thou wert there.
Or were I monarch o' the globe,   *of*
Wi' thee to reign, wi' thee to reign,   *With*
The brightest jewel in my crown
Wad be my queen, wad be my queen.   *Would*

Spooky stuff

As we know, Robert's mother, Agnes, and her home help, Betty Davidson, filled his head, and his imagination, with stories of the supernatural from a young age. Burns says of Betty:

She had, I suppose, the largest collection in the country of tales and songs concerning devils, ghosts, fairies, brownies, witches, warlocks, spunkies, kelpies, elf-candles, dead-lights, wraiths, apparitions, cantraips, giants, enchanted towers, dragons, and other trumpery.

The supernatural, and Robert's fascination with it, appears in many of his spooky masterpieces. No doubt Burns was attempting to ridicule superstition but he was also tapping into the beliefs of the Scottish country folk, especially their belief in the reality of Hell and its master, the Devil.

The Devil of Burns's work is no cartoon monster; he is the fallen angel who had declared war on God and a mighty power to be feared and respected. On the one hand we sense that Robert did not believe in the Devil; on the other he appears to be taking no chances.

But Burns didn't restrict his subjects or characters to Christian belief. Like all great writers and thinkers he borrowed from other cultures and ideologies. In his poetry he continually refers to gods and goddesses, mainly from Ancient Greece. This was a common poetic device long before Burns and is still in use. It's a rare poet who is not interested in myth, legend and folklore, and an even rarer reader who is not captivated and spellbound by them.

Boo!

TAM O'SHANTER

A Tale

'Of Brownyis and of Bogillis full is this Buke.'*Goblins, Demons, Book*
Gawin Douglas

When chapman billies leave the street,	*pedlars*
And drouthy neebors neebors meet;	*thirsty neighbours*
As market days are wearing late,	
And folk begin to tak the gate,	*take the road*
While we sit bousing at the nappy,	*drinking, ale*
An' getting fou and unco happy,	*And, drunk, very*
We think na on the lang Scots miles,	*not, long*
The mosses, waters, slaps and stiles,	*bogs, gaps*
That lie between us and our hame,	*hame*
Where sits our sulky, sullen dame,	
Gathering her brows like gathering storm,	
Nursing her wrath to keep it warm.	
This truth fand honest Tam o'Shanter,	*found, of*
As he frae Ayr ae night did canter:	*from, one*
(Auld Ayr, wham ne'er a town surpasses,	*Old, whom*
For honest men and bonie lasses).	*pretty*
O Tam! had'st thou but been sae wise,	*so*
As taen thy ain wife Kate's advice!	*taken, own*
She tauld thee weel thou was a skellum,	*told, well, scoundrel*
A blethering, blustering, drunken blellum;	*chattering, gossip*
That frae November till October,	
Ae market-day thou was na sober;	
That ilka melder wi' the Miller,	*each quantity of oats, with*
Thou sat as lang as thou had siller;	*silver(money)*
That ev'ry naig was ca'd a shoe on	*nag(horse), called*
The Smith and thee gat roarin fou on;	*got*
That at the Lord's house, ev'n on Sunday,	

Thou drank wi' Kirkton Jean till Monday;
She prophesied that late or soon,
Thou wad be found, deep drown'd in Doon, *would*
Or catch'd wi' warlocks in the mirk, *wizards, dark*
By Alloway's auld, haunted kirk. *church*

Ah, gentle dames! it gars me greet, *makes me cry*
To think how mony counsels sweet, *many*
How mony lengthen'd, sage advices,
The husband frae the wife despises!

But to our tale: – Ae market night,
Tam had got planted unco right,
Fast by the ingle, bleezing finely, *fireplace, blazing*
Wi' reaming swats that drank divinely; *foaming ale*
And at his elbow, Souter Johnie,
His ancient, trusty, drouthy crony: *friend*
Tam lo'ed him like a very brither; *loved, brother*
They had been fou for weeks thegither. *together*
The night drave on wi' sangs an' clatter; *drove, and*
And aye the ale was growing better: *always*
The Landlady and Tam grew gracious,
Wi' favours secret, sweet and precious:
The Souter tauld his queerest stories;
The Landlord's laugh was ready chorus:
The storm without might rair and rustle, *roar*
Tam did na mind the storm a whistle.

Care, mad to see a man sae happy,
E'en drown'd himsel amang the nappy. *among*
As bees flee hame wi' lades o' treasure, *fly, loads*
The minutes wing'd their way wi' pleasure:
Kings may be blest, but Tam was glorious,
O'er a' the ills o' life victorious! *all*

But pleasures are like poppies spread,
You seize the flow'r, its bloom is shed;
Or like the snow falls in the river,
A moment white – then melts for ever;
Or like the Borealis race,   *Northern Lights*
That flit ere you can point their place;
Or like the Rainbow's lovely form
Evanishing amid the storm. –
Nae man can tether Time nor Tide,   *No*
The hour approaches Tam maun ride;   *must*
That hour, o' night's black arch the key-stane,
That dreary hour he mounts his beast in;
And sic a night he taks the road in,   *such*
As ne'er poor sinner was abroad in.

The wind blew as 'twad blawn its last;   *it would*
The rattling showers rose on the blast;
The speedy gleams the darkness swallow'd;
Loud, deep, and lang the thunder bellow'd:
That night, a child might understand,
The Deil had business on his hand.   *Devil*

Weel-mounted on his grey mare Meg,
A better never lifted leg,
Tam skelpit on thro' dub and mire,   *rushed, puddle*
Despising wind, and rain, and fire;
Whiles holding fast his gude blue bonnett,   *good*
Whiles crooning o'er some auld Scots sonnet,
Whiles glow'rin round wi' prudent cares,
Lest bogles catch him unawares;   *goblins*
Kirk-Alloway was drawing nigh,
Where ghaists and houlets nightly cry.   *ghosts, owls*

By this time he was cross the ford,
Where in the snaw the chapman smoor'd; *snow, smothered*
And past the birks and meikle stane, *birches, big stone*
Where drunken Charlie brak's neck-bane; *broke his neck-bone*
And thro' the whins, and by the cairn, *gorse*
Where hunters fand the murder'd bairn; *found, child*
And near the thorn, aboon the well, *above*
Where Mungo's mither hang'd hersel'. *mother*
Before him Doon pours all his floods,
The doubling storm roars thro' the woods,
The lightnings flash from pole to pole,
Near and more near the thunders roll,
When, glimmering thro' the groaning trees,
Kirk-Alloway seem'd in a bleeze,
Thro' ilka bore the beams were glancing, *every hole*
And loud resounded mirth and dancing.

Inspiring bold John Barleycorn!
What dangers thou canst make us scorn!
Wi' tippeny, we fear nae evil; *twopenny beer*
Wi' usquabae, we'll face the devil! *whisky*
The swats sae ream'd in Tammie's noddle, *head*
Fair play, he car'd na deils a boddle, *farthing*
But Maggie stood, right sair astonish'd, *sore*
Till, by the heel and hand admonish'd,
She ventur'd forward on the light;
And wow! Tam saw an unco sight! *strange*

Warlocks and witches in a dance:
Nae cotillion, brent new frae France, *brand*
But hornpipes, jigs, strathspeys and reels,
Put life and mettle in their heels.

A winnock-bunker in the east,   *window seat*
There sat auld Nick, in shape o' beast;
A tousie tyke, black, grim, and large,   *shaggy dog*
To gie them music was his charge.
He screw'd the pipes and gart them skirl,   *made them shriek*
Till roof and rafters a' did dirl.   *rattle*
Coffins stood round, like open presses,   *cupboards*
That shaw'd the Dead in their last dresses;   *showed*
And (by some devilish cantraip sleight)   *magic trick*
Each in its cauld hand held a light.   *cold*
By which heroic Tam was able
To note upon the haly table,   *holy*
A murderer's banes, in gibbet-airns;   *bones, -irons*
Twa span-lang, wee, unchristened bairns;   *Two, small, babies*
A thief, new-cutted frae a rape,   *rope*
Wi' his last gasp his gab did gape;   *mouth*
Five tomahawks, wi' blude red-rusted: *blood*
Five scimitars, wi' murder crusted;
A garter which a babe had strangled:
A knife, a father's throat had mangled,
Whom his ain son of life bereft,   *own*
The grey hairs yet stack to the heft;   *stuck*
Wi' mair of horrible and awfu',
Which even to name wad be unlawfu'.   *would*

As Tammie glowr'd, amaz'd and curious,
The mirth and fun grew fast and furious;
The Piper loud and louder blew,
The dancers quick and quicker flew,
They reel'd, they set, they cross'd, they cleekit,   *grabbed*
Till ilka carlin swat and reekit,   *each witch sweated and steamed*
And coost her duddies to the wark,   *cast off her clothes*
And linkit at it in her sark!   *danced, shirt*

Now Tam, O Tam! had thae been queans, *they, girls*
A' plump and strapping in their teens!
Their sarks, instead o' creeshie flainen, *greasy cloth*
Been snaw-white seventeen-hunder linen! *snow, 1700 (fine thread)*
Thir breeks o' mine, my only pair, *breeches (trousers)*
That aince were plush, o' guid blue hair, *once, good*
wud hae gien them off my hurdies, *would, have given, backside*
For ae blink o' the bonie burdies! *one look, beautiful girls*
But wither'd beldams, auld and droll, *old*
Rigwoodie hags wad spean a foal, *Withered, abort*
Louping an' flinging on a crummock, *leaping, crooked staff*
I wonder did na turn thy stomach.

But Tam kent what was what fu' brawlie: *knew, full well*
There was ae winsome wench and wauli *jolly*
That night enlisted in the core, *crew*
Lang after ken'd on Carrick shore

(For mony a beast to dead she shot,
And perish'd mony a bonie boat,
And shook baith meikle corn and bear, *both, much, barley*
And kept the country-side in fear);
Her cutty sark, o' Paisley harn, *short shirt, coarse cloth*
That while a lassie she had worn,
In longitude tho' sorely scanty,
It was her best, and she was vauntie. *proud*
Ah! little ken'd thy reverend grannie,
That sark she coft for her wee Nannie, *bought*
Wi' twa pund Scots ('twas a' her riches), *pounds (money)*
Wad ever grac'd a dance of witches!

But here my Muse her wing maun cour, *must curb*
Sic flights are far beyond her power;
To sing how Nannie lap and flang *leaped and danced*

(A souple jade she was and strang),   *supple, strong*
And how Tam stood, like ane bewitch'd,
And thought his very een enrich'd: *eyes*
Even Satan glowr'd, and fidg'd fu' fain,   *fidgeted full of fondness*
And hotch'd and blew wi' might and main: *jerked*
Till first ae caper, syne anither,   *one, then another*
Tam tint his reason a' thegither,   *lost*
And roars out, 'Weel done, Cutty-sark!'
And in an instant all was dark:
And scarcely had he Maggie rallied,
When out the hellish legion sallied.

As bees bizz out wi' angry fyke,   *bother*
When plundering herds assail their byke;   *hive*
As open pussie's mortal foes,   *hare's*
When, pop! she starts before their nose;
As eager runs the market-crowd,
When 'Catch the thief!' resounds aloud;
So Maggie runs, the witches follow,
Wi' mony an eldritch skreich and hollo.   *unearthly*

Ah, Tam! Ah, Tam! thou'll get thy fairin!   *reward*
In hell they'll roast thee like a herrin!   *herring (fish)*
In vain thy Kate awaits thy comin!
Kate soon will be a woefu' woman!
Now, do thy speedy utmost, Meg,
And win the key-stane o' the brig;   *-stone, bridge*
There, at them thou thy tail may toss,
A running stream they dare na cross.
But ere the key-stane she could make,
The fient a tail she had to shake!   *not a*
For Nannie, far before the rest,
Hard upon noble Maggie prest,   *aim*
And flew at Tam wi' furious ettle;   *knew*

But little wist she Maggie's mettle!   *knew*
Ae spring brought off her master hale,   *whole*
But left behind her ain grey tale:
The carlin claught her by the rump, *witch clutched*
And left poor Maggie scarce a stump.

Now, wha this tale o' truth shall read,   *who*
Ilk man, and mother's son, take heed: *Each*
Whene'er to Drink you are inclin'd,
Or Cutty-sarks rin in your mind,   *run*
Think ye may buy the joys o'er dear;
Remember Tam o'Shanter's mare.

ON THE LATE CAPTAIN GROSE'S PEREGRINATIONS THROUGH SCOTLAND

Hear, Land o' Cakes, and brither Scots,	*of, brother*
Frae Maidenkirk to Johnie Groat's;-	*From*
If there's a hole in a' your coats,	*all*
I rede you tent it:	*advise, pay attention to*
A chield's amang you takin notes,	*fellow's among*
And, faith, he'll prent it:	*print*

If in your bounds ye chance to light	
Upon a fine, fat fodgel wight,	*good-humoured creature*
O' stature short, but genius bright,	
That's he, mark weel;	*well*
And wow! he has an unco sleight	*unusual skill*
O' cauk and keel.	*chalk and pencil (drawing)*

By some auld, houlet-haunted biggin,	*old, owl-, building*
Or kirk deserted by its riggin,	*roof*
It's ten to ane ye'll find him snug in	*one*
Some eldritch part,	*haunted*
Wi' deils, they say, Lord save's! colleaguin	*With devils,*
At some black art.	*save us, conferring*

	Each ghost,
Ilk ghaist that haunts auld ha' or chaumer,	*hall, chamber*
Ye gipsy-gang that deal in glamour,	*sorcery*
And you, deep-read in hell's black grammar,	
Warlocks and witches,	
Ye'll quake at his conjuring hammer,	
Ye midnight bitches.	

It's tauld he was a sodger bred,	*told, soldier*
And ane wad rather fa'n than fled;	*would, fallen*
But now he's quat the spurtle-blade,	*quit, swordstick*
And dog-skin wallet,	
And taen the Antiquarian trade,	*taken*
I think they call it.	

He has a fouth o' auld nick-nackets:	*fund, nick-nacks*
Rusty airn caps and jinglin jackets,	*iron, armour*
Wad haud the Lothians three in tackets,	*hold, shoenails,*
A towmont gude;	*twelvemonth(year), good*
And parritch-pats and auld saut-backets,	*porridge-pots,*
Before the Flood.	*salt-buckets*

Of Eve's first fire he has a cinder;	
Auld Tubalcain's* fire-shool and fender;	*-shovel*
That which distinguished the gender	
O' Balaam's ass:	
A broomstick o' the witch of Endor,	
Weel shod wi' brass.	*Well*

Forbye, he'll shape you aff fu' gleg	*Besides, off full smart*
The cut of Adam's philibeg;	*small kilt*
The knife that nickit Abel's craig	*cut, throat*
He'll prove you fully,	
It was a faulding jocteleg,	*folding penknife*
Or lang-kail gullie.	*long kale knife*

But wad ye see him in his glee,	
For meikle glee and fun has he,	*much*
Then set him down, and twa or three	*two*
Gude fellows wi' him:	*Good*
And port, O port! shine thou a wee,	*little*
And Then ye'll see him!	

Now, by the Pow'rs o' verse and prose!
Thou art a dainty chield, O Grose!
Whae'er o' thee shall ill suppose,   *Whoever*
They sair misca' thee;   *sore miscall*
I'd take the rascal by the nose,
Wad say, 'Shame fa' thee!'   *befall*

Tubalcain, Balaam, Abel and Adam are Old Testament characters.

EPITAPH FOR MR WILLIAM MICHIE

Schoolmaster of Cleish Parish, Fifeshire

Here lie Willie Michie's banes;   *bones*
O Satan, when ye tak him,   *take*
Gie him the schulin o' your weans,   *Give, schooling of, children*
For clever deils he'll mak them!   *devils, make*

ADDRESS TO THE DEIL

O THOU! whatever title suit thee
Auld Hornie, Satan, Nick, or Clootie*,
Wha in yon cavern, grim an' sootie,   *Who, yonder, and*
Clos'd under hatches,
Spairges about the brunstane cootie,   *splashes, brimstone dish*
To scaud poor wretches!   *scald*

Hear me, auld Hangie, for a wee,   *old Hangman*
An' let poor damned bodies be;
I'm sure sma' pleasure it can gie,   *small, give*
Ev'n to a deil,   *devil*
To skelp an' scaud poor dogs like me,   *spank*
An' hear us squeel!

Great is thy pow'r an' great thy fame;
Far kenn'd an' noted is thy name;   *known*
An' tho' yon lowin heugh's thy hame,   *flaming hollow, home*
Thou travels far;
An' faith! thou's neither lag nor lame,   *slow*
Nor blate nor scaur.   *bashful, afraid*

Whyles, ranging like a roarin lion,   *Now*
For prey, a' holes an' corners tryin;
Whyles, on the strong-wing'd tempest flyin,
Tirlin' the kirks;   *stripping*
Whyles, in the human bosom pryin,
Unseen thou lurks.

*Old Scottish nickname for the devil, meaning cloven-hooved

I've heard my rev'rend grannie say,
In lanely glens ye like to stray;   *lonely*
Or where auld ruin'd castles grey
Nod to the moon,
Ye fright the nightly wand'rer's way
Wi' eldritch croon.   *With unearthly*

When twilight did my grannie summon
To say her pray'rs, douce, honest woman!   *sober*
Aft 'yont the dike she's heard you bummin,   *Often beyond,*
Wi' eerie drone;   *humming*
Or, rustlin thro' the boortrees comin,   *elder bush*
Wi' heavy groan.

Ae dreary, windy, winter night,   *One*
The stars shot down wi' sklentin light,   *slanting*
Wi' you mysel I gat a fright,   *got*
Ayont the lough;   *beyond, pond*
Ye like a rash-buss stood in sight,   *clump of rushes*
Wi' waving sugh.   *moan*

The cudgel in my nieve did shake,   *fist*
Each bristl'd hair stood like a stake,
When wi' an eldritch, stoor 'Quaick, quaick,'   *deep-voiced*
Amang the springs,   *Among*
Awa ye squatter'd like a drake,   *Away*
On whistling wings.

Let warlocks grim, an' wither'd hags,
Tell how wi' you, on ragweed nags,   *ragwort*
They skim the muirs an' dizzy crags   *moors*
Wi' wicked speed;
And in kirk-yards renew their leagues,
Owre howket dead.   *Over dug-up*

Thence, countra wives, wi' toil an' pain
May plunge an' plunge the kirn in vain;   *milk churn*
For oh! the yellow treasure's taen   *taken*
By witchin skill;
An' dawtet, twal-pint hawkie's gaen *petted, twelve-pint cow gone*
As yell's the bill.   *dry as the bull*

Thence, mystic knots mak great abuse   *make*
On young guidmen, fond, keen, an' croose; *husbands, cocky*
When the best wark-lume i' the house,   *work tool in*
By cantraip wit,   *magic*
Is instant made no worth a louse,
Just at the bit.   *the nick of time*

When thowes dissolve the snawy hoord, *thaws, snowy hoard*
An' float the jinglin icy boord,   *surface*
Then water-kelpies haunt the foord *water-spirits, ford*
By your direction,
An' nighted trav'llers are allur'd   *benighted*
To their destruction.

And aft your moss-traversing spunkies *bog-crossing sprites*
Decoy the wight that late an' drunk is: *strong*
The bleezin, curst, mischievous monkies   *blazing*
Delude his eyes,
Till in some miry slough he sunk is,
Ne'er mair to rise.   *more*

When masons' mystic word an' grip
In storms an' tempests raise you up,
Some cock or cat your rage maun stop,   *must*
Or, strange to tell!
The youngest brither ye wad whip
Aff straught to hell!   *Off straight*

Lang syne, in Eden's bonie yard, *long ago, garden*
When youthfu' lovers first were pair'd,
An' all the soul of love they shar'd,
The raptur'd hour,
Sweet on the fragrant flow'ry swaird, *turf*
In shady bow'r;

Then you, ye auld snick-drawin dog! *scheming*
Ye cam to Paradise incog,
An' play'd on man a cursèd brogue, *trick*
(Black be your fa'!) *lot*
An' gied the infant warld a shog, *gave, world, shake*
Maist ruin'd a'. *Almost, all*

D'ye mind that day, when in a bizz, *bustle*
Wi' reeket duds an reestet gizz, *smoky, scorched wig*
Ye did present your smootie phiz *smutty face*
'Mang better folk, *Among*
An' sklented on the man of Uzz *squinted on Job*
Your spitefu' joke? *(Old Testament Prophet)*

An' how ye gat him i' your thrall, *got*
An' brak him out o' house and hal', *broke, hold*
While scabs and blotches did him gall,
Wi' bitter claw;
An' lows'd his ill-tongued, wicked scaul, *untied, scolding wife*
Was warst ava? *worse of all*

But a' your doings to rehearse,
Your wily snares an' fechtin fierce, *fighting*
Sin' that day Michael did you pierce, *Since, Archangel Michael*
Down to this time,
Wad ding a Lallan tongue, or Erse, *Be too much for,*
In prose or rhyme. *Lowland, Irish*

An' now, Auld Cloots, I ken ye're thinkin,   *know*
A certain bardie's rantin, drinkin,   *merrymaking*
Some luckless hour will send him linkin,   *hurrying*
To your black pit;
But faith! he'll turn a corner jinkin,   *dodging*
An' cheat you yet.

But fare you weel, auld Nickie-ben!
O wad ye tak a thought an' men'!
Ye aiblins might, I dinna ken,   *perhaps, don't know*
Still hae a stake:
I'm wae to think upo' yon den,   *sad*
Ev'n for your sake!

EPITAPH FOR HOLY WILLIE

Here Holy Willie's sair worn clay   *sore*
Taks up its last abode;   *Takes*
His saul has ta'en some other way,   *soul, taken*
I fear, the left-hand road.

Stop! there he is, as sur's a gun,   *sure's*
Poor, silly body, see him;
Nae wonder he's as black's the grun,   *No, ground*
Observe wha's standing wi' him.   *who's, with*

Your brunstane devilship, I see,   *brimstone*
Has got him there before ye;
But haud your nine-tail cat a wee   *hold*
Till ance you've heard my story.   *once*

Your pity I will not implore,
For pity ye have nane;   *none*
Justice, alas! has gi'en him o'er,   *given*
And mercy's day is gane.   *gone*

But hear me, Sir, deil as ye are,   *devil*
Look something to your credit;
A coof like him wad stain your name,   *fool, would*
If it were kent ye did it.   *known*

THE DEIL'S AWA WI' THE EXCISEMAN

The deil cam fiddlin' thro' the town,   *devil came*
And danc'd awa wi' th' Exciseman,   *away with, Taxman*
And ilka wife cries, 'Auld Mahoun,   *each, Old Devil*
I wish you luck o' the prize, man.'   *of*

Chorus
The deil's awa, the deil's awa,
The deil's awa wi' the Exciseman,
He's danc'd awa, he's danc'd awa,
He's danc'd awa wi' the Exciseman.

We'll mak our maut, and we'll brew our drink,   *make, malt*
We'll laugh, sing, and rejoice, man,
And mony braw thanks to the meikle black deil, *many fine,*
That danc'd awa wi' th' Exciseman.   *big*

There's threesome reels, there's foursome reels,
There's hornpipes and strathspeys, man,
But the ae best dance ere came to the land   *one*
Was the deil's awa wi' the Exciseman.

EPIGRAM ADDRESSED TO AN ARTIST

Whom the poet found engaged on a representation of Jacob's dream

Dear – , I'll gie ye some advice, *give*
You'll tak it no uncivil: *take it not*
You shouldna paint at angels mair, *should not, more*
But try and paint the devil.

To paint an Angel's kittle wark, *hard work*
Wi' Nick, there's little danger: *With*
You'll easy draw a lang-kent face, *long-known*
But no sae weel a Stranger. *so well*

Natural wonders

As a son of the soil and a farmer himself for part of his adult life, it's not surprising that Robert Burns would write about the natural world, or the environment as we would call it today.

He's deservedly acknowledged as a 'nature poet', yet there's a strange contradiction in the work of Burns. Landscape plays little part in his poetry and songs. While he refers to the specific things within a landscape like rivers, flowers, animals and birds, he never describes the view. Perhaps, he was too captivated by detail to bother about the bigger picture.

That said, his work contains some of the greatest descriptions and celebrations of nature ever written. 'To a Mouse', for example, is one of the most sensitive works in literature – the first line alone is one of the best known and most endlessly quoted of Burns's poems. Like much of his poetry, it was inspired by an incident he personally witnessed, on this occasion when he was ploughing a field.

Reading the poem today, and the many others that Burns wrote about nature and the great outdoors, instantly connects us to the beauty, peacefulness, pleasures and, at times, harshness of the countryside. Two centuries after they were written, they remain a breath of fresh air.

TO A MOUSE

Wee, sleeket, cowrin, tim'rous beastie,	*Little, sleek, small beast*
Oh, what a panic's in thy breastie!	*small breast*
Thou need na start awa sae hasty	*not, away so*
Wi' bickerin brattle!	*With hurrying scamper*
I wad be laith to rin an' chase thee	*would, loath, run*
Wi' murd'ring pattle!	*paddle (board from the plough)*

I'm truly sorry man's dominion	
Has broken Nature's social union,	
An' justifies that ill opinion	*And*
Which makes thee startle	
At me, thy poor earth-born companion,	
An' fellow-mortal!	

I doubt na, whyles, but thou may thieve:	*at times*
What then? poor beastie, thou maun live!	*must*
A daimen icker in a thrave	*occasional ear of corn, sheaf*
'S a sma' request;	*Is, small*
I'll get a blessin wi' the lave,	*what's left*
An' never miss 't!	

Thy wee bit housie, too, in ruin!	*small house*
Its silly wa's the win's are strewin!	*walls, winds*
An' naething, now, to big a new ane,	*nothing, build, one*
O' foggage green!	*coarse grass*
An' bleak December's winds ensuin	
Baith snell an' keen!	*Both, biting cold*

Thou saw the fields laid bare an' waste,	
An' weary winter comin fast,	
An' cozie here beneath the blast	
Thou thought to dwell,	
Till crash! the cruel coulter past	*ploughshare*
Out thro' thy cell.	

That wee bit heap o' leaves an' stibble   *stubble*
Has cost thee monie a weary nibble!   *many*
Now thou's turn'd out for a' thy trouble,
But house or hald,   *Without, a holding*
To thole the winter's sleety dribble   *endure*
An' cranreuch cauld!   *hoar frost, cold*

But, Mousie, thou art no thy lane   *not alone*
In proving foresight may be vain:
The best laid schemes o' mice an' men
Gang aft agley,   *Often go awry*
An' lea'e us nought but grief an' pain   *leave*
For promis'd joy.

Still thou art blest, compar'd wi' me!
The present only toucheth thee:
But, och! I backward cast my e'e   *oh!, eye*
On prospects drear!
An' forward, tho' I canna see,
I guess an' fear!

MY FATHER WAS A FARMER

My father was a farmer upon the Carrick border, O,
And carefully he bred me in decency and order, O;
He bade me act a manly part, though I had ne'er a farthing, O;
For without an honest manly heart, no man was worth regarding, O.

Then out into the world my course I did determine, O;
Tho' to be rich was not my wish, yet to be great was charming, O;
My talents they were not the worst, nor yet my education, O:
Resolv'd was I at least to try to mend my situation, O.

In many a way, and vain essay, I courted Fortune's favour, O;
Some cause unseen still stept between, to frustrate each endeavour, O;
Sometimes by foes I was o'erpower'd, sometimes by friends forsaken, O;
And when my hope was at the top, I still was worst mistaken, O.

Then sore harass'd and tir'd at last, with Fortune's vain delusion, O,
I dropt my schemes, like idle dreams, and came to this conclusion, O;
The past was bad, and the future hid, its good or ill untried, O;
But the present hour was in my pow'r, and so I would enjoy it, O.

No help, nor hope, nor view had I, nor person to befriend me, O;
So I must toil, and sweat, and moil, and labour to sustain me, O;
To plough and sow, to reap and mow, my father bred me early, O;
For one, he said, to labour bred, was a match for Fortune fairly, O.

Thus all obscure, unknown, and poor, thro' life I'm doom'd to wander, O,
Till down my weary bones I lay in everlasting slumber, O:
No view nor care, but shun whate'er might breed me pain or sorrow, O;
I live to-day as well's I may, regardless of to-morrow, O.

But cheerful still, I am as well as a monarch in his palace, O,
Tho' Fortune's frown still hunts me down, with all her wonted malice, O:
I make indeed my daily bread, but ne'er can make it farther, O:
But as daily bread is all I need, I do not much regard her, O.

When sometimes by my labour, I earn a little money, O,
Some unforeseen misfortune comes gen'rally upon me, O;
Mischance, mistake, or by neglect, or my goodnatur'd folly, O:
But come what will, I've sworn it still, I'll ne'er be melancholy, O.

All you who follow wealth and power with unremitting ardour, O,
The more in this you look for bliss, you leave your view the farther, O
Had you the wealth Potosi* boasts, or nations to adore you, O,
A cheerful honest-hearted clown I will prefer before you, O.

*Potosi is a city in Bolivia, South America,
which at the time was famous for its wealth in silver.*

ON SEEING A WOUNDED HARE LIMP BY ME

Inhuman man! curse on thy barb'rous art,
And blasted by thy murder-aiming eye;
May never pity soothe thee with a sigh,
Nor never pleasure glad thy cruel heart!

Go live, poor wanderer of the wood and field,
The bitter little of life that remains!
No more the thickening brakes and verdant plains
To thee shall home, or food, or pastime yield.

Seek, mangled wretch, some place of wonted rest,
No more of rest, but now of dying bed!
The sheltering rushes whistling o'er thy head,
The cold earth with thy bloody bosom Crest.

Oft as by winding Nith* I, musing, wait
The sober eve, or hail the cheerful dawn,
I'll miss thee sporting o'er the dewy lawn,
And curse the ruffian's aim, and mourn thy hapless fate.

The River Nith is in Dumfries and Galloway, south-west Scotland.

TO A MOUNTAIN DAISY

Wee, modest, crimson-tippèd flow'r,   *Small*
Thou's met me in an evil hour;
For I maun crush amang the stoure   *must, among, dust*
Thy slender stem:
To spare thee now is past my pow'r,
Thou bonie gem.   *beautiful*

Alas! it's no thy neibor sweet,   *not, neighbour*
The bonie lark, companion meet,
Bending thee 'mang the dewy weet   *among, wet*
Wi' spreckl'd breast,   *With speckled*
When upward-springing, blythe, to greet
The purpling East.

Cauld blew the bitter-biting north   *cold*
Upon thy early, humble birth;
Yet cheerfully thou glinted forth
Amid the storm,
Scarce rear'd above the parent-earth
Thy tender form.

The flaunting flowers our gardens yield
High shelt'ring woods an' wa's maun shield: *and walls must*
But thou, beneath the random bield   *shelter*
O' clod or stane,   *Of, stone*
Adorns the histie stibble-field   *dry and stony, stubble*
Unseen, alane.   *alone*

There, in thy scanty mantle clad,
Thy snawie-bosom sun-ward spread,   *snowy-*
Thou lifts thy unassuming head
In humble guise;
But now the share upteárs thy bed,
And low thou lies!

Such is the fate of artless maid,
Sweet flow'ret of the rural shade!
By love's simplicity betray'd
And guileless trust;
Till she, like thee, all soil'd, is laid
Low i' the dust.   *in*

Such is the fate of simple bard,
On life's rough ocean luckless starr'd!
Unskilful he to note the card
Of prudent lore,
Till billows rage and gales blow hard,
And whelm him o'er!

Such fate to suffering Worth is giv'n,
Who long with wants and woes has striv'n,
By human pride or cunning driv'n
To mis'ry's brink;
Till, wrench'd of ev'ry stay but Heav'n,
He ruin'd sink!

Ev'n thou who mourn'st the Daisy's fate,
That fate is thine--no distant date;
Stern Ruin's ploughshare drives elate,
Full on thy bloom,
Till crush'd beneath the furrow's weight
Shall be thy doom.

THE LEA RIG

When o'er the hill the eastern star
Tells bughtin time is near, my jo, *penning sheep, darling*
And owsen frae the furrow'd field *oxen from*
Return sae dowf and weary O; *so dull*
Down by the burn, where scented birks
Wi' dew are hangin clear, my jo, *With*
I'll meet thee on the lea-rig, *strip of field left fallow or unploughed*
My ain kind Dearie O. *own*

At midnight hour, in mirkest glen, *darkest*
I'd rove, and ne'er be eerie, O, *afraid*
If thro' that glen I gaed to thee, *went*
My ain kind Dearie O;
Altho' the night were ne'er sae wild,
And I were ne'er sae weary O,
I'll meet thee on the lea-rig,
My ain kind Dearie O.

The hunter lo'es the morning sun; *loves*
To rouse the mountain deer, my jo;
At noon the fisher seeks the glen
Adown the burn to steer, my jo:
Gie me the hour o' gloamin' grey, *Give, of twilight*
It maks my heart sae cheery O, *makes*
To meet thee on the lea-rig,
My ain kind Dearie O.

WINTER: A DIRGE

The wintry west extends his blast,
And hail and rain does blaw;   *blow*
Or the stormy north sends driving forth
The blinding sleet and snaw: *snow*
While, tumbling brown, the burn comes down,
And roars frae bank to brae;   *from, hill*
And bird and beast in covert rest,
And pass the heartless day.

'The sweeping blast, the sky o'ercast,'
The joyless winter day
Let others fear, to me more dear
Than all the pride of May:
The tempest's howl, it soothes my soul,
My griefs it seems to join;
The leafless trees my fancy please,
Their fate resembles mine!

Thou Power Supreme, whose mighty scheme
These woes of mine fulfil,
Here firm I rest; they must be best,
Because they are Thy will!
Then all I want – O do Thou grant
This one request of mine! –
Since to enjoy Thou dost deny,
Assist me to resign.

TO A LOUSE

On Seeing One on a Lady's Bonnet at Church

Ha! whare ye gaun' ye crowlin ferlie?	*Where, going, crawling wonder*
Your impudence protects you sairly;	*sorely*
I canna say but ye strunt rarely	*strut*
Owre gauze and lace,	*Over*
Tho faith! I fear ye dine but sparely	*In truth*
On sic a place.	*such*

Ye ugly, creepin, blastit wonner,	*worthless creature*
Detested, shunn'd by saunt an sinner,	*saint*
How daur ye set your fit upon her--	*dare*
Sae fine a lady!	*So*
Gae somewhere else, and seek your dinner	*Go*
On some poor body.	

Swith! in some beggar's haffet squattle;	*Off!, head squat*
There ye may creep, and sprawl, and sprattle;	*scramble*
Wi' ither kindred, jumping cattle;	
In shoals and nations;	
Whare horn nor bane ne'er daur unsettle	*Where, bone, dare*
Your thick plantations.	

Now haud you there! ye're out o' sight,	*hold*
Below the fatt'rils, snug an tight,	*ends of ribbon*
Na, faith ye yet! ye'll no be right,	
Till ye've got on it --	
The vera tapmost, tow'rin height	*very topmost*
O' Miss's bonnet.	

My sooth! right bauld ye set your nose out,   *bold*
As plump an grey as onie grozet: *any gooseberry*
O for some rank, mercurial rozet,   *resin*
Or fell, red smeddum,   *poisonous powder*
I'd gie you sic a hearty dose o't,   *give, such, of it*
Wad dress your droddum!   *Would, backside*

I wad na been surpris'd to spy   *not*
You on an auld wife's flainen toy   *old, flannel hat*
Or aiblins some bit duddie boy,   *perhaps, small ragged*
On's wyliecoat;   *undervest*
But Miss's fine Lunardi!* fye!
How daur ye do't?   *dare*

O Jeany, dinna toss your head,   *don't*
An set your beauties a' abroad!   *abroad*
Ye little ken what cursed speed   *know*
The blastie's makin!   *nuisance*
Thae winks an finger-ends, I dread,   *Those, and*
Are notice takin!

O wad some Power the giftie gie us   *gift*
To see oursels as ithers see us!   *ourselves, others*
It wad frae monie a blunder free us   *from many*
An foolish notion:
What airs in dress an gait wad lea'e us,   *leave*
An ev'n devotion!

* bonnet in the style of Lunardi's flying balloon

Poetry of life

From everyday occurrences to special occasions, personal experiences to momentous events, Robert Burns recorded and retold life in his time.

Never one to stand on ceremony, he delighted in poking fun at others, as in poems such as 'Willie Wastle' and 'Address to the Unco Guid'. He was equally good at laughing at himself. In 'Rantin, Rovin, Robin' Burns celebrates his birth and even predicts his success and mark on the world.

Like all poets, Burns also wrote about the things that moved him. He cared deeply about the political consequences of the union of Scotland and

England, particularly the exploitation of those who had gained financially at the expense of the Scottish people and their culture. 'Scots Wha Hae' is a passionate rallying call for national identity and pride.

But love of his country was only part of a far greater emotion: the love of his fellow human beings. In poems like 'A Man's A Man For a' That' and 'The Rights of Woman', Burns shows us that brotherly and sisterly love, mutual respect and concern for others are far better measures of a person than riches or titles.

Whatever the inspiration, however short or long the poem, he uses words to paint a vivid picture of many aspects of life that are still as relevant today as they were two centuries ago. The true mark of a master wordsmith is the ability to say in a few words what we feel physically and emotionally. There are few who can do this better than Robert Burns.

RANTIN, ROVIN, ROBIN

There was a lad was born in Kyle,
But whatna day o' whatna style,   *what, of*
I doubt it's hardly worth the while
To be sae nice wi' Robin.   *so, with*

Robin was a rovin boy,
Rantin, rovin, rantin, rovin,   *Free*
Robin was a rovin boy,
Rantin, rovin Robin!

Our monarch's hindmost year but ane   *one*
Was five-and-twenty days begun,
'Twas then a blast o' Janwar win'   *of January wind*
Blew hansel in on Robin.   *a gift*

The gossip keekit in his loof,   *peeped, palm*
Quo' scho, 'Wha lives will see the proof,   *Quote she, who*
This waly boy will be nae coof: *goodly, no fool*
I think we'll ca' him Robin.'   *call*

'He'll hae misfortunes great an' sma',   *have, and small*
But ay a heart aboon them a'   *always, above, all*
He'll be a credit till us a',
We'll a' be proud o' Robin.'   *of*

'But sure as three times three mak nine,   *make*
I see by ilka score and line   *each*
This chat will dearly like our kin',
So leeze me on thee, Robin!'   *blessings*

SELKIRK GRACE

Some hae meat and canna eat	*have, cannot*
And some wad eat that want it:	*would*
But we hae meat and we can eat,	
Sae let the Lord be thankit.	*So, thanked*

TO A HAGGIS

Fair fa' your honest, sonsie face	*Good luck to, cheerful*
Great Chieftain o' the Puddin-race!	*of*
Aboon them a' ye tak your place,	*above, all, take*
Painch, tripe, or thairm	*Paunch, guts*
Weel are ye wordy o' a grace	*Well, worthy*
As lang's my arm.	*long*

The groaning trencher there ye fill,
Your hurdies like a distant hill, *buttocks*
Your pin wad help to mend a mill *skewer would*
In time o' need,
While thro' your pores the dews distil
Like amber bead.

His knife see Rustic-labour dight, *wipe*
An' cut you up wi' ready sleight, *And, with, skill*
Trenching your gushing entrails bright, *Digging*
Like onie ditch; *any*
And then, O what a glorious sight,
Warm-reekin rich. *steaming*

Then, horn for horn they stretch an' strive, *horn-spoon*
Deil tak the hindmost, on they drive *Devil take the last,*
Till a' their weel-swall'd kytes belyve *well-swollen bellies soon*
Are bent like drums;
Then auld Guidman, maist like to ryve, *old, almost, burst*
'Bethankit' hums. *murmurs 'God be thanked'*

Is there that owre his French ragout, *over*
Or olio that wad staw a sow, *sicken*
Or fricassee wad mak her spew *make*
Wi' perfect sconner, *disgust*
Looks down wi' sneering, scornfu' view
On sic a dinner? *such*

Poor devil! see him owre his trash,
As feckless as a wither'd rash, *rush (water plant)*
His spindle shank a guid whip-lash, *thin leg, good*
His nieve a nit; *closed fist, nut*
Thro' bluidy flood or field to dash, *bloody*
O how unfit!

But mark the Rustic, haggis-fed,
The trembling earth resounds his tread;
Clap in his walie nieve a blade,   *large fist*
He'll mak it whissle;   *whistle*
An' legs, an' arms, an' heads will sned,   *lop off*
Like taps o' thrissle.   *tops of thistle*

Ye Pow'rs wha mak mankind your care
And dish them out their bill o' fare,
Auld Scotland wants nae skinking ware   *watery stuff*
That jaups in luggies;   *splashes in bowls*
But if ye wish her gratefu' prayer,
Gie her a Haggis!   *Give*

A MAN'S A MAN FOR A' THAT

Is there for honest Poverty
That hings his head, an' a' that?   *hangs, and all*
The coward slave, we pass him by,
We dare be poor for a' that!
For a' that, an' a' that,
Our toils obscure, an' a' that,
The rank is but the guinea's stamp
The Man's the gowd for a' that   *gold*

What though on hamely fare we dine,   *homely food*
Wear hodden grey, an' a' that?   *rough woollen cloth*
Gie fools their silks and knaves their wine,   *Give*
A Man's a Man for a' that.
For a' that, an' a' that,
Their tinsel show, an' a' that,
The honest man, tho' e're sae poor,   *so*
Is king o' men for a' that!

Ye see yon birkie ca'd a lord,   *yonder fellow called*
Wha struts, an stares, an' a' that,   *Who*
Though hundreds worship at his word,
He's but a cuif for a' that.   *fool*
For a' that, an' a' that,
His ribband, star an' a' that,
The man of independent mind
He looks and laughs at a' that.

A prince can mak a belted knight,   *make*
A marquis, duke an' a' that!
But an honest man's aboon his might   *above*
Guid faith, he mauna faa that!   *must not befall*
For a' that, an' a' that,
Their dignities, an' a' that,
The pith o' sense and pride o' worth,
Are higher rank than a' that!

Then let us pray that come it may,
As come it will for a' that
That Sense and Worth, o'er a' the earth,
May bear the gree, and a' that.   *be most important*
For a' that, an' a' that,
Its comin' yet for a' that
That Man to Man, the world o'er,
Shall brothers be for a' that!

THE RIGHTS OF WOMAN

While Europe's eye is fix'd on mighty things,
The fate of Empires and the fall of Kings;
While quacks of State must each produce his plan,
And even children lisp the *Rights of Man*;
Amid this mighty fuss just let me mention,
The *Rights of Woman* merit some attention.

First, in the Sexes' intermix'd connection,
One sacred Right of Woman is, protection:
The tender flower that lifts its head, elate,
Helpless, must fall before the blasts of Fate,
Sunk on the earth, defac'd its lovely form,
Unless your shelter ward th' impending storm.

Our second Right-but needless here is caution,
To keep that right inviolate's the fashion;
Each man of sense has it so full before him,
He'd die before he'd wrong it – 'tis decorum:
There was, indeed, in far less polish'd days,
A time, when rough rude man had naughty ways,
Would swagger, swear, get drunk, kick up a riot,
Nay even thus invade a Lady's quiet.

Now, thank our stars! those Gothic times are fled;
Now, well-bred men – and you are all well-bred –
Most justly think (and we are much the gainers)
Such conduct neither spirit, wit, nor manners.

For Right the third, our last, our best, our dearest,
That right to fluttering female hearts the nearest;
Which even the Rights of Kings, in low prostration,
Most humbly own – 'tis dear, dear admiration!
In that blest sphere alone we live and move;
There taste that life of life-immortal love.
Smiles, glances, sighs, tears, fits, flirtations, airs;
'Gainst such an host what flinty savage dares,
When awful Beauty joins with all her charms –
Who is so rash as rise in rebel arms?

But truce with kings, and truce with constitutions,
With bloody armaments and revolutions;
Let Majesty your first attention summon,
Ah! ça ira! THE MAJESTY OF WOMAN!

ADDRESS TO THE TOOTHACHE

My curse upon your venom'd stang,	*sting*
That shoots my tortur'd gums alang,	*along*
And thro' my lug gies mony a twang,	*ear gives many, twinge*
Wi' gnawing vengeance,	*With*
Tearing my nerves wi' bitter pang,	
Like racking engines!	

When fevers burn, or ague freezes,
Rheumatics gnaw, or colic squeezes,
Our neebour's sympathy can ease us,   *neighbour's*
Wi' pitying moan;
But thee!, thou hell o' a' diseases,   *of all*
They mock our groan!

Adown my beard the slavers trickle,   *All down, saliva*
I throw the wee stools o'er the mickle,
As round the fire the giglets keckle,   *youngsters cackle*
To see me loup;   *leap*
An' raving mad, I wish a heckle   *And, comb for dressing flax*
Were i' their doup!   *in, backside*

O' a' the num'rous human dools,   *woes*
Ill-hair'sts, daft bargains, cutty-stools *bad harvests, stools of repentance*
Or worthy frien's rak'd i' the mools,   *friends laid in the earth*
Sad sight to see!
The tricks o' knaves, or fash o' fools,   *annoyance*
Thou bear'st the gree!   *takes the prize*

Where'er that place be priests ca' hell,   *call*
Where a' the tones o' misery yell,
An' rankèd plagues their numbers tell,
In dreadfu' raw,   *row*
Thou, Tooth-ache, surely bear'st the bell
Amang them a'!   *Among*

O thou grim, mischief-making chiel,   *fellow*
That gars the notes of discord squeel,   *makes*
Till daft mankind aft dance a reel
In gore a shoe-thick,
Gie a' the faes o' Scotland's weal   *Give, foes*
A towmond's toothache!   *twelve-month's*

WILLIE WASTLE

Willie Wastle dwalt on Tweed,	*dwelt*
The spot they ca'd it Linkumdoddie.	*called*
Willie was a wabster guid	*weaver good*
Could stown a clue wi onie body.	*have stolen, with any*
He had a wife was dour and din,	*sulky, ill-coloured*
O, Tinkler Maidgie was her mither!	*Tinker, mother*
Sic a wife as Willie had,	*such*
I wad na gie a button for her.	*would not give*

She has an e'e (she has but ane),	*eye*
The cat has twa the very colour,	*two*
Five rusty teeth, forbye a stump,	*as well as*
A clapper-tongue wad deave a miller;	*deafen*
A whiskin beard about her mou,	*mouth*
Her nose and chin they threaten ither:	*each other*
Sic a wife as Willie had,	
I wad na gie a button for her.	

She's bow-hough'd, she's hem-shin'd,	*bandy-legged, crooked shins*
Ae limpin leg a hand-breed shorter;	*One, hand's-breadth*
She's twisted right, she's twisted left,	
To balance fair in ilka quarter;	*each*
She has a hump upon her breast,	
The twin o' that upon her shouther	*shoulder*
Sic a wife as Willie had,	
I wad na gie a button for her.	

Auld baudrans by the ingle sits,	*Old cat, fire*
An wi her loof her face a-washin;	*with, paw*
But Willie's wife is nae sae trig,	*not so trim*
She dights her frunzie wi a hushion;	*wipes, nose, footless sock*
Her walie nieves like midden-creels,	*large fists, manure-baskets*
Her face wad fyle the Logan Water:	*would foul*
Sic a wife as Willie had,	
I wad na gie a button for her.	

EPIGRAM ON MISS DAVIES

On being asked why she had been formed so little,
and Mrs. A . . . so big

Ask why God made the gem so small?
And why so huge the granite?
Because God meant mankind should set
That higher value on it.

ADDRESS TO THE UNCO GUID, OR THE RIGIDLY RIGHTEOUS

My Son, these maxims make a rule,
An' lump them ay thegither;   *And, always together*
The Rigid Righteous is a fool,
The Rigid Wise anither: *another*
The cleanest corn that e're was dight   *thrashed*
May hae some pyles o' caff in;   *have, grains of chaff*
So ne'er a fellow creature slight
For random fits o' daffin.   *larking about*

                    Solomon. Ecclesiastes chapter 7, verse 16

O ye wha are sae guid yoursel,   *who, so good yourself*
Sae pious and sae holy,
Ye've nought to do but mark and tell
Your neebour's fauts and folly!   *neighbour's faults*
Whase life is like a weel-gaun mill,   *whose, well-going*
Supply'd wi' store o' water;   *with*
The heapèt happer's ebbing still,   *heaped hopper*
An' still the clap plays clatter.   *mill clapper*

Hear me, ye venerable core,   *folk*
As counsel for poor mortals
That frequent pass douce Wisdom's door,   *sober / grave*
For glaikit Folly's portals;   *foolish*
I, for their thoughtless, careless sakes,
Would here propone defences,   *propose*
Their donsie tricks, their black mistakes,   *unlucky*
Their failings and mischances.

Ye see your state wi' theirs compar'd,
And shudder at the niffer;   *comparison*
But cast a moment's fair regard,
What maks the mighty differ?   *makes*
Discount what scant occasion gave,
That purity ye pride in;
And (what's aft mair than a' the lave)   *often more, rest*
Your better art o' hidin.

Think, when your castigated pulse
Gies now and then a wallop,   *Gives, plunge*
What ragings must his veins convulse,
That still eternal gallop!
Wi' wind and tide fair i' your tail,   *in*
Right on ye scud your sea-way;
But in the teeth o' baith to sail,   *both*
It maks an unco lee-way.   *uncommon*

See Social Life and Glee sit down,
All joyous and unthinking,
Till, quite transmugrify'd, they're grown
Debauchery and Drinking:
O would they stay to calculate
Th' eternal consequences;
Or your more dreaded hell to state,
Damnation of expenses!

Ye high, exalted, virtuous dames,
Tied up in godly laces,
Before ye gie poor Frailty names,
Suppose a change o' cases;
A dear-lov'd lad, convenience snug,
A treach'rous inclination,
But let me whisper i' your lug,   *ear*
Ye're aiblins nae temptation.   *perhaps no*

Then gently scan your brother man,
Still gentler sister woman;
Tho' they may gang a kennin wrang,   *go, little wrong*
To step aside is human:
One point must still be greatly dark,
The moving Why they do it;
And just as lamely can ye mark,
How far perhaps they rue it.

Who made the heart, 'tis He alone
Decidedly can try us;
He knows each chord, its various tone,
Each spring, its various bias:
Then at the balance let's be mute,
We never can adjust it;
What's done we partly may
compute,
But know not what's resisted.

CROWDIE EVER MAIR

O that I had ne'er been married,
I wad never had nae care,   *would, no*
Now I've gotten wife an' weans,   *and children*
An' they cry 'Crowdie' ever mair.   *Porridge, evermore*

Chorus
Ance crowdie, twice crowdie,   *Once*
Three times crowdie in a day
Gin ye crowdie ony mair,   *If, any more*
Ye'll crowdie a' my meal away.

Waefu' Want and Hunger fley me,   *Woeful, terrify*
Glowrin' by the hallan en';   *staring, cottage doorway*
Sair I fecht them at the door,   *Sore, fought*
But aye I'm eerie they come ben.   *always, fearful, inside*

SCOTS WHA HAE

Scots, wha hae wi Wallace bled,   *who have with*
Scots, wham Bruce has aften led,   *whom, often*
Welcome to your gory bed
Or to victorie!
Now's the day, and now's the hour:
See the front o' battle lour,   *of, menace*
See approach proud Edward's power –
Chains and slaverie!

Wha will be a traitor knave?   *Who*
Wha can fill a coward's grave?
Wha sae base as be a slave?   *so*
Let him turn, and flee!
Wha for Scotland's King and Law
Freedom's sword will strongly draw,
Freeman stand, or Freeman fa',   *fall*
Let him follow me!

By Oppression's woes and pains,
By your sons in servile chains,
We will drain your dearest veins,
But they shall be free!
Lay the proud usurpers low!
Tyrants fall in every foe!
Liberty's in every blow! –
Let us do, or die!

AULD LANG SYNE

Should auld acquaintance be forgot,   *old*
And never brought to mind?
Should auld acquaintance be forgot,
And auld lang syne!   *long ago*

Chorus
For auld land syne, my dear,
For auld lang syne,
We'll tak a cup o' kindness yet,   *take, of*
For auld lang syne.

And surely ye'll be your pint-stowp!   *pint-measure*
And surely I'll be mine!
And we'll tak a cup o' kindness yet,
For auld lang syne.

We twa hae run about the braes,   *two have, hills*
And pou'd the gowans fine;   *pulled, daisies*
But we've wander'd mony a weary fit   *many, foot*
Sin' auld lang syne.   *Since*

We twa hae paidl'd in the burn,   *waded, stream*
Frae morning sun till dine;   *From breakfast until dinner*
But seas between us braid hae roar'd   *broad, have*
Sin' auld lang syne.

And there's a hand, my trusty fiere!   *companion*
And gie's a hand o' thine!   *give*
And we'll tak' a right gude-willie waught,   *good-will drink*
For auld lang syne.

THE LAND OF BURNS

Many of the places where Robert Burns lived and worked can be visited. A number of sites have been acquired by the National Trust for Scotland and others have been preserved and enhanced by the local authority in cooperation with the Scottish Tourist Board. Anyone wishing to know more of Burns and the Land o' Burns should visit or write to the Scottish Tourist Board in Edinburgh. The Board publishes a number of attractive pamphlets on Burns and is responsible for developing the Burns Heritage Trail – a tour of the places linked with Scotland's greatest poet – and some of these places are listed here.

Alloway

The cottage where Robert Burns was born still stands and can be visited. Joined to the house is a museum with a major collection of relics. Alloway Kirk, where Tam o' Shanter saw the witches dance, is about half a mile from the cottage and was already a ruin in Burns' day. William Burnes, the poet's father, is buried there. Nearby is the Tam O' Shanter Experience, part of the Burns National

Heritage Park. Its displays and audiovisual shows bring to life the works and times of Burns. The Auld Brig o' Doon, which crosses the river, is believed to be 700 years old. It is the bridge over which Tam made his escape from the witches. Alongside is the Burns Monument, completed in 1823, which contains more relics of the poet.

Ayr

Burns' statue stands outside the railway station and nearby in the High Street is the Tam o' Shanter Inn – the starting point for Tam's ride. The Auld Brig mentioned in the poem 'The Brigs of Ayr' (not included in this selection) is still in use for pedestrians. The house in Sandgate where young Robert was tutored for three weeks by John Murdoch is commemorated by a tablet. Burns was baptised at the Auld Kirk in Ayr.

Brow

The little hamlet on the Solway Coast which in Burns' time had an unfounded reputation as a spa. Shortly before he died, Burns was sent here by his doctor and friend, James Maxwell, in the hope that sea-bathing might be beneficial to his health.

Dumfries

The ancient Bridge House and the Burgh Museum have relics of the poet. Burns' first Dumfries home

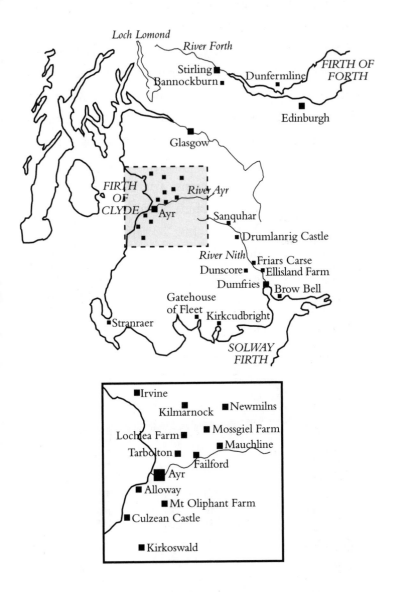

in the Wee Vennel (now Bank Street) is not open to the public. His second and larger home in Mill Vennel (now Burns Street) is a leading Burns Museum. His wife, Jean Armour, lived here until her death in 1834. Burns was buried in St Michael's Churchyard. On 19 September 1815, his remains were transferred to a vault under a mausoleum erected to his memory. The churchyard holds numerous graves of Burns' friends. In a narrow passage leading off the High Street is the Globe Inn, described by Burns as his 'favourite howff'. The relics include his chair and an inscribed window pane. The Theatre Royal, visited frequently by Burns, is due to be reconstructed but it will keep its original frontage.

Burn's second and larger home at Dumfries in Mill Vennel

Eglinton Woods

Off the main road between Irvine and Kilwinning, are Eglinton Castle, Park and Woods (which cover 50 acres), owned and maintained by the local authority. There is a small statue of Burns in the park, supposedly marking the spot where Richard Brown urged Burns to send his verses to a magazine for publication.

Ellisland Farm

This hundred-acre farm to which Burns moved in June 1788 is on the west bank of the Nith about six miles north of Dumfries on the A76. Ellisland was farmed until 1921, when it was bought by a former president of the Edinburgh Burns Club and given to the nation. It is preserved as a working farm and the restored granary includes an exhibition that gives a vivid image of Burns' life as a farmer and shows how he tried to introduce new farming methods.

Failford

Due south of Lochlea on the A758 is a memorial to Burns' 'Highland Mary' (Mary Campbell of Auchnamore). It is in the centre of the village at the spot over the Fail Water where Burns and Mary are said to have parted for the last time with an exchange of vows.

Gatehouse of Fleet

In the Murray Arms Hotel a room may be seen where Burns probably wrote 'Scots, Wha Hae'.

Irvine

Here Robert and Gilbert Burns went in 1781 to learn flax dressing. They lodged in a house in Glasgow Vennel, now marked by a plaque. The Irvine Burns Club, founded 2 June 1826, is one of the oldest in the world and has a very interesting museum.

Two of its founder members were personal friends of Burns: Dr John MacKenzie and David Sillar. The club rooms are situated in a house called Wellwood in Eglinton Street and are open to the public.

Kilmarnock

Here the first Kilmarnock Edition of Burns' poems was published by John Wilson; the site of his premises is marked by a plaque. Dean Castle, formerly the home of Burns' friend, the Earl of Glencairn, now has an attractive garden and a notable collection of musical instruments. In Kay Park, the Burns Monument is a red sandstone temple surmounted by a tower which contains a good museum of Burnsiana.

Kirkcudbright

In the Selkirk Arms (Inn), it is believed Burns wrote the Selkirk Grace, sometimes still used (see p 103).

Kirkoswald

Souter Johnnie's House, built in 1785, is a National Trust for Scotland property. It is a museum with furniture of Burns' day and the implements of a village cobbler. In the garden are four amusing life-size figures of Tam o' Shanter, Souter Johnnie, the innkeeper and his wife. They were made in 1802 by James Thom, a self-taught sculptor from Tarbolton.

Largs

An unusual monument to the bard is the Burns Garden at Douglas Park which has been laid out in an attempt to retell the story of the life and works of the great Scottish poet. One part of the garden relates the tale of Tam o' Shanter and there are replicas of famous Alloway landmarks.

Lochlea Farm

This farm was the home of the Burns family from 1777 until 1784 and it lies about a mile north of the B744, halfway between Tarbolton and Mauchline. The present buildings are not the ones lived in by Burns.

Mauchline

A major centre of Burns interest. Burns is said to have met Jean Armour on the green by Mauchline Burn. Burns House, a museum in Castle Street, is where he took a room for Jean in 1788 and where the couple lived for a few months before the move to Ellisland. Burns and Jean were married in Gavin Hamilton's house which adjoins the fifteenth-century tower of Mauchline Castle. Auld Nance Tinnock's Tavern that was once the Sma' Inn (now no longer an inn) is opposite.

Poosie Nansie's Tavern in Mauchline

Mauchline Churchyard (the present church was built in 1829) contains the graves of four of Burns' children and some of his friends, including Gavin Hamilton and Willie Fisher (Holy Willie). Opposite the church is Poosie Nansie's Tavern, an ale shop and lodging house in Burns' time. You can still have a drink there. The revels witnessed by Burns resulted in the poem 'The Jolly Beggars'. On the outskirts of the town, at the junction of the A76 and the B744, stands the National Burns Memorial Tower in which there is a small museum.

Mossgiel Farm

The farm rented by the Burns brothers in 1783. At the Burns National Memorial fork left onto the Tarbolton road and the farm, which has since been rebuilt, is on the right.

Mount Oliphant

William Burnes moved here with his family in 1766. The farm, which is still worked today but with a neighbouring farm, stands on high ground one and a half miles southeast of Alloway. It commands magnificent views of Arran and the Ayrshire coast.

Tarbolton

Here is the seventeenth-century house, now owned by the National Trust for Scotland, where Burns attended dancing classes in 1779, founded the Bachelors' Club with his friends in 1780, and was installed as a mason in 1781. Willie's Mill (Tarbolton Mill) is just outside Tarbolton on the road to Lochlea. In Burns' day it was the home of his close friend William Muir. When Jean Armour was thrown out of her home because of her association with Burns she found shelter with Muir. It was also the setting for Burns' satirical poem 'Death and Doctor Horn-brook' (not included in this selection).